INDEPENDENT
BOOKSTORE
PLANNING & DESIGN

INDEPENDENT
BOOKSTORE
PLANNING & DESIGN

By KEN WHITE, ISP
and FRANK WHITE, ISP

ST. FRANCIS PUBLICATIONS
Westwood, N.J.

To Tom and Deanna, Gary and Tammy, Amy, Jill, Jennifer and Lauren, Max, Kyle and Zachary, John and Helen, Jeffrey and Taylor, Matthew and Joseph. Inspirations all.

First published in the United States of America in 1992 by St. Francis Publications, Inc. 7 James St., Westwood, NJ 07675.

Library of Congress Cataloging-in-Publication Data

White, Ken, ISP and White, Frank, ISP

Independent Bookstore Planning & Design

1. Book industries and trade--Management.
2. Booksellers and bookselling--Management.
3. Planning, design, merchandising and
   construction.
4. Real Estate--site location.

Includes glossary and index.

ISBN 0-9625457-1-6

92-0644-57 CIP Card No.

Printed and Bound in Hong Kong.

CONTENTS

PREFACE

The purpose of this book is threefold. First, it is a complete reference book on independent bookstore planning and design. Second, it is a guide through the myriad activities and details the new booksellers will face. It chronicles the steps to properly and effectively plan, open, reposition, or modernize an independent bookstore. Third, and most important, it introduces new ways to position new bookstores in the market, with new PDM (planning, design, and merchandising) concepts that have a proven success record. These concepts surpass most other bookselling strategies now in use anywhere in the English-speaking world.

If you are a prospective bookseller and burning to open a great bookstore, perhaps this book will change your life, and ours! At least it should sharpen our mutual understanding of bookselling in the 1990s. We say "our," because we write for ourselves as well as for you. So, when we say "we," we mean ourselves and you the bookseller. "We" are the three of us planning a store together.

This book is both a beginner's and a professional bookseller's self-help reference; it is the bookstore planning and design Bible. However, this book is also written for anyone who simply wants to read and gain a little knowledge about bookstore planning and design.

This book is a sequel to BOOKSTORE PLANNING & DESIGN, published in 1982. We have heard time and again that the 1982 edition was useful for many of the 7,500 new bookstores planned and opened in the United States since then- up from 10,000 to 17,500 in the past decade. It is the latest, most comprehensive, and up-to-date reference in the field of retail bookselling.

INDEPENDENT BOOKSTORE PLANNING & DE-SIGN is meant to be an energizer - a battery charger that will be of particular value to those who would like to reorganize, renovate, or otherwise upgrade their facilities: to introduce a new look, to create a new image, to revamp their style, or to put a faster spin on their visual merchandising program. Whether you are most interested in a new, second-hand, or out-of-print store, a superstore, a kiosk, a children's store, or any other type of specialty bookstore, we believe that a wide variety of readers will find this book clear, concise, and helpful.

If you are both serious and fortunate enough to be able to open an independent bookstore, it is essential for you to prepare yourself, to know, before you start, how to "market position" your new store, how to prepare a market segmentation plan, a mission statement, a retail mix trade off, competitive positioning and differentiation (words new to our Glossary) in your new store. This book provides benchmarks to show you the way.

Much of INDEPENDENT BOOKSTORE PLANNING & DESIGN focuses on the importance and the need for individualized merchandising concepts. These are concepts you must consider to position your new store for the particular niche or market opening you have chosen and, at the same time, not find yourself a sitting duck for the next round of competition to come along.

To that end, this book is a compilation of current marketing insights: bookselling know-how, merchandising strategies, store planning, image statements, and design elements essential to the creation of successful and enduring bookstore designs. Elaboration on elements included in this book can stimulate you to make a creative and positive impact on the design of future independent bookstores.

This book describes the importance of selecting the right neighborhood, trends in site location, store lease terms, build-out allowances, the cost of building or renovating and opening a new bookstore - all essential things for you to be aware of. The job ahead will not always be easy. An eye-opening and informative Tenant Criteria statement used by landlords and developers of large strip centers and regional malls to describe the working relationships between landlords, tenants, their architects, and design consultants is provided in Appendix II. It is absolutely essential reading for you as a bookseller before you sign a long-term lease for retail store space.

This book is more than a fact checker. It puts the spotlight on the trend toward incorporating customer comfort features. Features such as clean customer restrooms, baby-changing stations, fireplaces, comfortable chairs, music, review tables, color concepts, and graphics are among many of the new topics addressed in this rule book for bookselling.

Detail follows detail as numerous plans and photographs are used to illustrate, beyond a mere record of fact, a range of up-market, mid-market, and discount bookstores. New superstores (extra-large, service-oriented bookstores), the bookselling phenomenon of the 1990s, are also illustrated. The plan diagrams of both independent and four of the largest national chain superstores are also presented for a better understanding of this new phenomenon.

Many types of independent Christian, Children's, Museum, Information Center, Law, Medical, Military, Government, College and Futuristic Comic Book Stores are presented here for the first time.

A wide range of bookstore design styles, from chic, refined, up-market shops to rough-and-tumble second-hand center-city stores are included. The basic elements that enter into the process of creating these retail bookselling environments are illustrated.

Striking storefronts, outside signs, a well-balanced floor plan with well-defined traffic patterns, properly sized sections and adjacencies, and appropriate book categories tuned to the same beat as the demographics of your market are features that must be right for successful book retailing in the 1990s. Techniques by which these elements can be imaginatively integrated into the plan of successful bookstores are recounted throughout the book.

Intense stuff! And the functional cash wraps, work stations, back rooms, office arrangement, use of flexible store fixturing, and new store fixture-design directions also described in this book are even more so. Merchandise inserts for children's flats, magazines, and maps; provisions for installing CRT's, computers, music systems, and security devices; floor covering strategies; and trends in lighting and ceiling design, color, decor, signing and graphics are just a few of the diverse image-building elements illustrated and described in this book.

Use this book as a road map - never mind how long it takes - to set a direction for your new bookstore. Use the ideas that apply to your situation. Be creative and innovative. Approach and develop the design of your independent bookstore with enthusiasm. Seek out and engage the most experienced professional help to join your team, to work with you to develop and finalize your position statement, mission statement, competitive analysis, site location, budgets, proforma statements, merchandise planning, interior design, and store architecture.

This book points out the value of joining forces with a professional bookstore planner/management-advisor to combine his or her experience with yours. The task of analyzing your market opportunities, combining a variety of PDM elements, creating a marketing strategy, and developing a marvelous look for your new bookstore is complex and time consuming. Working with a professional bookstore planner/management advisor will take a load off your shoulders at a time when there are hundreds of new book industry topics and operational bits and pieces for you to digest and comprehend. This team approach brings the best minds together to strengthen the creative planning and imaginative marketing efforts for your new store.

This is the only book that takes you into some of the most successful independent bookstores in the U.S., Canada, and the Far East - many types of specialized general trade bookstores, small and large, show you how each combines the many elements that make a successful bookstore...A place where good *book merchandising* can be practiced!

With nearly 300 illustrations, including 100 in full color, the volume details not just the how, but the why of choosing the kind of store to open, the store's site, merchandise profile, cost and inventory requirements, size and atmosphere, arriving at a merchandise plan and design concept, drawing, designing the floors, walls and ceilings, selecting the fixtures and materials, lighting, communication systems, color, signage and graphic systems, and all other physical elements that contribute to *better book merchandising*.

The final purpose of this book is to record the body of bookstore planning knowledge employed for the opening of many successful bookstores in the immediate past and to lay a foundation for those planned into the year 2000.

We are indebted to our colleagues, clients, and managers - far too numerous to mention - who allowed us to photograph their stores and reviewed this manuscript, and whose astute comments considerably contributed to the quality of this book and its fit to booksellers' needs.

Both our company's and our personal visions of retail bookselling have, over the past decade, grown with the industry. We have expanded our view and understanding of how bookstores work, and of the kind of bookstore management, the high seriousness of financial matters, marketing, planning, operation, and design it will take to succeed in the 1990s. And that leads us back to basics, where one saying holds true.

"Bookstore business planning, space planning, design, and visual merchandising is an art - no matter where or by whom it is practiced."

How is it possible to know where to begin? We would like to say, "This is the place to start - there is no time or place better." To those who will accept the challenge of planning and merchandising wonderful bookstores, we say, "welcome to an exciting experience." Read the book and let's get started! Our future is right now.

Ken White, ISP *Westwood, New Jersey*
Frank White, ISP *Columbus, Ohio*

PART ONE

INTRODUCTION

The primary purpose of Part One is to develop in the reader an awareness of the many activities involved in conceptualizing, locating, planning, building or modernizing, and opening a new bookstore. Part One defines types of bookstores, the nature of their locations, and types of contextual and classical design themes that are successful.

Part One is also intended to establish for the reader an awareness of the importance of developing a Planning, Design, and Merchandising (PDM) program. It also explains the roles of the store planner, the architect, and for larger projects, the planning team.

Finally, Part One examines, in depth, techniques that are employed to conceptualize design ideas that lead to innovative profit planning. Four chapters are devoted to the elements of bookstore interior, exterior, and graphics design. Chapter 11 explains the technique of putting it all together, and takes us through the preparation of the final project construction plans to the new bookstore opening.

Part One is comprehensive, descriptive, and visual. It attempts to convey an understanding of why successful independent and institutional retail bookstores, small and large children's stores, general and specialty shops, and super bookstores follow the planning sequences described. It spreads the future of special kinds of bookselling before us in a living blueprint for a better way to be a quality, independent bookseller.

CHAPTER 1

PREPARATION FOR PLANNING

It has been said that books are the treasured wealth of mankind. That vision continues to be borne out literally as well as figuratively: bookstore sales in the United States grew by a billion dollars a year between 1896 and 1991.[1] More books are sold in the United States than in any other country in the world.

How to Get Into the Bookstore Business

There are three basic ways to open a bookstore.

Option 1   Start from scratch. Lease, plan, design, merchandise, and open a new store.

Option 2   Buy an existing bookstore business. Bookstore businesses for sale are regularly advertised in *The American Booksellers Association* (ABA) *Newswire, The American Bookseller, Publishers Weekly,* and state and regional Booksellers Association newsletters.

Option 3   Buy a bookstore business franchise from one of several national and regional franchise bookstore groups. Franchise organizations provide worthwhile advice to help you with the details of opening and operating quality bookstores.

Who Buys Books?

Just about anybody who can read buys books. Books are sold to men, women, and children of every description. Books are bought for enjoyment, education, entertainment, relaxation, self-improvement, information, self-help, as gifts, and for hundreds of other reasons.

Customers who make up the largest segment of the book-buying population have unique characteristics, as portrayed in Table 1.1. Data culled from new census material provide a detailed snapshot of typical book buyers after a decade of unprecedented growth.

Customers buy books of every classification in hundreds of subject categories, from normal- and large-format hardbound books to trade and mass-market paperbacks, College students buy new and used textbooks, reference works,

The warmth and appeal of this mall superstore is evident to customers even before they enter. Paneled and glazed wood entrance doors are part of the store's new image.
Webster's Books, Lansing, Mich.

general fiction, and non-fiction trade books. Business and professional people, and people in the military and government buy and read an enormous number of specialized reference books.

Customers interested in do-it-yourself and home improvement, linguistics, public speaking, writing, and trivia buy almanacs and thesauruses and auto repair manuals. People interested in art, photography, travel, religion, history, cooking, gardening, collecting, music, and literature buy all kinds of English and foreign language books and dictionaries.

Grandmothers, grandfathers, moms, dads and just about everybody else in the family buys a children's book for a specific purpose (coloring, computers) or as a light-hearted gift at one time or another. People who buy books also buy maps, globes, magazines, newspapers, comic books, baseball cards, video tapes, and audio books.

The adage that there is a book published (or about to be released) on every subject and a customer for every book is probably true. People buy literally tons of remainders, publishers' overstock, hurt books, used hard- and soft-bound books, fictional books, magazines, and newspapers. People buy books one at a time, in stocks and piles, by complete series, and sometimes, to fill a new law library.

Many customers form attachments to their local bookstores. They come to regard them as "their place," a place they can depend on to have the books they need or the willingness to order the book for delivery as soon as possible.

Exterior view of one of Berkeley, Calif.'s, favorite independent bookstores. The Black Oak.

Table 1.1   Characteristics of Typical Book-Buying Customers

- They have higher household incomes than the average. The 1990 Census showed the U.S. population at 249,870,000, with a median household income of $29,317. 53% of book buyers have an annual household income of $30,000 or over.

- The majority of book buyers are slightly older than the average. The median age of the population in 1990 was 33. The median age of the largest segment of book buyers was 35 - 49.

- Book buyers are better educated than the average. 61% of the book-buying population are college graduates. 31% are high school only graduates. And 8% attended or completed only elementary school.

- They are more literate than the average.

- They buy more books, both in units and dollars, than the average.

    - 6 in 10 adults (63%) buy at least 1 book in any 3 month period.

    - The average adult buys 3.7 books in any 3 month period.

    - About 1 in 4 adults (26%) buys 5 or more books in any 3 month period.

    - About 1 in 6 adults (17%) buys 3 - 4 books in any 3 month period.

    - About 1 in 5 adults (20%) buys 1 - 2 books in any 3 month period.

- They are more likely than the average to be female: 56% women versus 44% men. (37% of women are not employed, but 48% work full time, and 14% part time.)

In large measure, the current demographics data underlie and expand on trends. There are vast numbers of book buyers at every economic level who are unique; they prefer different kinds of bookstores and buy and read different categories of books.

Retail Bookstore Market Segmentation

The retail bookstore business is made up of hundreds of market segments. The question is, which individual or combination of market segments are needed to support the specialty or general bookstore that we propose to open. Determining which segment, or segments, of the market are best for us begins with analyzing the demographics of the particular market and analyzing the competition that currently serves that market. Demographic profiles are available from the ABA.[2]

Demographic Profiles and Site Location Analysis

The ABA bookstore site-location analysis service will provide a specially prepared, three-page Demographic Profile, generated for you by one of the country's best-known marketing organizations. From its up-to-date computer data bank, the report will include:

- Population - current year and five-year projection
- Households for the same time period
- Median value and rent
- Age of persons
- Family size
- Sex and marital status
- Income distribution for households and families
- Vehicles available
- Labor force
- Occupation
- Education
- Race

Entrance to Wyckoff, N.J.'s, favorite independent bookseller. The Book Nook.

These custom studies describe the affluence, education, occupation, and mobility of our trading area's level of resident population, factors that can influence our bookstore's success. Along with the Demographic Profile, ABA will supply an explanation of the data categories (*not* a critique of an individual site).

With the demographic profile in hand, walk the neighborhood, and visit the site on different days and at different hours. Take a look at what happens when it rains or snows. Is there any traffic on the street after 9 P.M.? Talk to your potential business neighbors and ask about the neighborhood and shopping patterns.

Once you have digested the demographic data available to you, the best way to prepare yourself for planning is to write down a summary of the key points on which you intend to proceed. Read it aloud, look at it, and revise it as many times as necessary to establish a Mission Statement for the new store.

Mission Statement

A Mission Statement is a description of the proposed store, its place in the community, the type of customers you wish to attract, the type of books the store will focus on, and the services the store promises to deliver. Preparation of a Mission Statement will help you arrive at a clear picture of the new store. Mission Statements are useful for communicating your concept to prospective lenders, for describing your goals and objectives to prospective employees, and in preparation of the planning, design, and merchandising specifications we will discuss in Chapter 3. A quality Mission Statement also is applicable to your publicity and promotional activities.

The Mission Statement will vary with each individual bookstore. Table 1.2 provides an example of a Mission Statement for new and remodeled stores (see also Appendix II).

Assume that we are planning to open an up-market, general bookstore. The name for this example will be *The Successful Bookstore*. Our first determination must be to seriously decide to the extent possible what kind of store *The Successful Bookstore* will be. We will have to determine requirements similar to the criteria shown in Table 1.2.

Front-of-store merchandise presentation. A Clean Well Lighted Book Store, San Francisco, Calif.

Table 1.2 Mission Statement 1:
What *The Successful Bookstore* Will Be

The Successful Bookstore will be the dominant upscale book retailer in the community we serve.

We will achieve market dominance by meeting or exceeding our customers' expectations, by providing them with **"the thinking person's book store."**

The **"thinking person's bookstore"** will be characterized by having:

- Knowledgeable people who provide superior service, and
- who are supported by accurate, timely, and responsive systems, in
- a store that is intelligently laid out and signed, and that
- presents merchandise in an exciting, inviting, and comfortable environment, and
- represents assortments that are well selected and balanced, both qualitatively and quantitatively, to meet our customers' needs.
- Our professional staff, our new store design, our operating policies and procedures, and the books selected - their presentation and promotion - will consistently reinforce our targeted customer's self-image.

Our success will be judged by both our sales and profitability, which will be superior, and also by the fact that we will become:

- The preferred place for upscale book buyers to shop,
- while also being the preferred employer among upscale book stores, and
- the upscale bookstore preferred by the real book-buying community in our city.

The Mission Statement now describes the manner in which we intend to present ourselves - whether we are a new, second-hand, or general bookstore, or a unique, niche, or specialty bookstore. It is important in this segmentation process to define how our new store will be different. Once this vision is clear to us, we can clearly say what *The Successful Bookstore* will *not* be! Table 1.3 provides some examples.

Table 1.3 Mission Statement 2:
What *The Successful Bookstore* Will Not Be

- An ordinary bookstore.
- A discount operation.
- A self-service/low-service operation.
- A bookstore that focuses primarily on low-end juvenile books, commercial fiction, mass-market, bargain books, or other low-end products.
- A merchandiser of the following categories: role playing, series romance, horror, true crime, men's adventure, pornography, westerns, or occult (if titles in any of these categories have significant demand by targeted customers, they will be stocked).
- Positioned as either an elitist or downmarket merchant from the point of view of its assortment or its prototypical store design.
- A merchandiser only of frontlist books. Backlist will be represented in all of our categories; however, backlist will not be *The Successful Bookstore*'s merchandising thrust.
- A merchandiser of faddish non-book products. *The Successful Bookstore* will represent neither high nor low-priced side lines.

Having established who we are and who we are not, what do we want customers to think of us? What customer response do we seek to evoke?

Customer Response Statement For *The Successful Bookstore*

The Successful Bookstore is, for me, the right books, in the right edition, with the right service, right now!

To achieve the bookstore business described, we must be prepared to make certain retail mix trade-offs that will make *The Successful Bookstore* unique and segmented from the competition established in our trade area.

Retail Mix Trade-Offs

In retailing today, the customer is asked to trade off specific operational attributes of retail mix (value, service, and selection) by each competitor. Selecting which attributes to stress and which to de-emphasize provides the foundation for defining *The Successful Bookstore's* differentiating characteristics in the Mission Statement.

A high brick tower provides an effective background for an exterior sign. Taylors Bookstore, Dallas, Texas.

Table 1.4   Relevant Attributes for Book Retailers

Competitive Bookstore's feature:

Personal Service	Breadth/Depth of Inventory
Selection	Promotional Program
Ambiance	PDM (Planning, Design, and
Customer Services	Merchandising) Strategies

Customers of *The Successful Bookstore* will be asked to trade off *price* (we will not discount from list price), *breadth* of selection (we will not be a superstore), and *depth* of selection (we will not be a mass-merchant), in exchange for more personalized services.

Table 1.5   Example of Retail Mix Trade-Offs

Personal Service

We will:

- Treat each customer as our patron and not as if he or she is an inconvenience.

Selection

We will:

- In key categories, offer at least 20 percent more titles than the current independent and chain bookstore competitors.

- Tailor the quality of assortments to the needs of targeted customers across and within markets.

- Showcase assortments with current titles focusing on "the new and the now."

- Emphasize hardcover and tradepaper editions as opposed to mass-market and bargain books; however, appropriate mass-market driven categories will be supported.

The Promotional Strategy of *The Successful Bookstore*

Our promotional strategy will revolve around titles, authors, categories, and themes that focus on our positioning, merchandise thrust, and targeted customers' interests. We will primarily promote frontlist titles but selectively incorporate backlist titles when appropriate. We will encourage handselling books by our staff.

The Successful Bookstore also will tie promotions into literary/book category awards. Our promotional strategy will be seasonally tuned, following the retail calendar, while also being sensitive to international, domestic, regional, and local market trends.

Front of Store Focus

Our Front of Store (lease-line) Statement will be designed to consistently reinforce our positioning, our customers' interests, and our strengths. Front of Store Statements will always include an array of titles that revolve around *the new and the now* theme.

Recently reviewed books receiving either national or local spotlighting and of interest to our targeted customers will be displayed with either the actual review or with excerpts from the review or dust jacket.

Merchandising Strategy: Key Categories

Our new store will concentrate its energies on bookselling. The key book categories around which *The Successful Bookstore* will drive its business are included in Table 1.6.

Multi-level, general bookstore. Cody's, Berkeley, Calif.

Table 1.6   Key Book and Non-Book Categories

Category	Percent Inventory
Fiction	16.25%
Mystery/Suspense	4.00
Current Affairs	2.80
History	4.00
Biography	4.25
Travel	9.50
Performing Arts	2.50
Fine Arts	3.80
Cooking	4.95
Business and Computer	8.40
Life-Style/Leisure Activities	7.00
Juvenile	9.75
General Reference	3.50
Psychology	3.25
Humor	2.80
Family/Childcare	1.25
Sidelines	12.00
Magazines	2.50
Calendars	4.25
Books/Related Non-Books	5.25
	100.00%

Establishing our merchandising strategy by key categories helps to identify the amount of space that we will dedicate to each section to adequately stock the categories listed.

Sidewalk sales at Allan Weiner's antiquarian, new and used book and compact disc store. Academy Bookstore, New York City.

Specialized feature book category selections will include:

Regional/Local Interest	Award Winning Titles
Local Authors	First Authors Program
Small Pleasures	Special Editions/Bindings
Gift Books	Books on Tape

Categories that will be represented, but not emphasized, in *The Successful Bookstore* will include:

Non-Series Romance	Westerns
Science Fiction/Fantasy	Large Print
Horror	Reference
Religion/Bibles/Philosophy	Belles Lettres
Nature/Science/Pets	Literary Criticism
Exercise/Fitness/	Poetry
Diet/Health/Beauty	Transportation
Addiction and Recovery	New Age/Astrology
True Crime	Computer Software

Remainder and Promotional Books

Remainders and promotional books will be stocked. The selection will concentrate on appropriate titles and price points within most of our key categories:

Fiction	Lifestyle/Leisure Activities
Mystery/Suspense	History
Performing Arts	Fine Arts
Humor	Cooking
Business	Juvenile
Travel	Regional/Local Interest
General Reference	Current Affairs
Cars/Trains/Planes & Ships	Biography

The Successful Bookstore's merchandise emphasis will be on hard-cover and trade paperbacks as well as on better price points. Some limited editions, special boxed sets, and slip-case editions of selected titles within key categories will be displayed in a special section.

Keep in mind that this example describes hypothetical stock requirements of *The Successful Bookstore*. Each store is unique. The stock requirements for each store must be tailored to its individual location (see Appendix II).

This listing may be supplemented by additional features of our particular store such as the addition of periodicals, journals, magazines, monographs, and other specialty reading materials. Let us now think about the look of our store, the ambiance we will create.

Ambiance

Ambiance is the single word used to sum up the total look of our new store. The ambiance we will create includes the points indicated in Table 1.7.

Table 1.7   Ambiance
• Store design will be appealing to the upmarket but not be pretentious; it will be comfortable, inviting, and accessible.
• Directional signage will be clear and informative.
• Lighting will accentuate products and complement the color palette.
• The store design will be contemporary or updated traditional in its design elements so that it is perceived as up-to-date, but not faddish.
• Visual merchandising, product displays, promotional themes, and programs will focus on the right books at the right time, in the right section, and all be supported with the right signage.
• An attempt will be made to have important books for targeted customers first or at least with competitive parity.
• The staff's dress code will reflect positioning.

In the above section, a clear picture of visual style, display objectives, merchandising strategy, and staff appearance has been established. This is, however, only a suggestive outline. The mission statement of each store is unique in every respect.

Store Services

The unique combination of store services that we put into place will be extremely important in building a solid business with staying power. The schedule of services that *The Successful Bookstore* will offer include those presented in Table 1.8.

Store Design Approach

To create *The Successful Bookstore* design ambiance, we will use the design theories of visual appeal, customer circulation, flexibility, and merchandise layout further discussed in Chapters 4 and 5.

Design theories are underlying principles, systems of assumption, procedures, speculations, and ideas agreed upon - about bookstore functions, market appeal, and operation. Bookstore design theories have been developed to formulate, apply, and evaluate essential design elements and principles to meet sales objectives,

Baskets of books and promotional dumps combine to create a warm front of visual merchandising, greeting and a sense of hospitality at this independent superstore. LIBERTIES Fine Books & Music, Boca Raton, Fla.

Table 1.8   Bookstore Services

Basic Services

- Gift certificates, special accounts, business accounts, institutional charges, magazine, and special newspaper subscriptions will be available.

- An attempt will be made to special order all domestic titles in print or to assist customers in obtaining requested books.

- Customers will be able to access the store by phone or fax.

- Merchandise purchased will be shipped anywhere for customers.

- Gift wrapping will be free for purchases made by customers.

- An attempt will be made to provide an out-of-print search service.

- There will be policies and procedures, and marketing programs, that facilitate institutional, organizational, and corporate account development and retention.

  - The basic services description can be further evaluated, as follows.

  - *Mail order:* Customer requests (if in stock) will be mailed when they have paid for the book. We will send customers information as to availability and cost. Customers can save time and call in advance for this information.

  - *Special orders:* Special orders means that books the customer requests will be ordered in a special shipment from the publisher or wholesaler. We will have a computer system with information on our wholesaler's warehouse inventory along with shipment and delivery times from the publisher.

  - *Catalogue orders:* The Successful Bookstore's catalogue will be a customized reprint of our wholesaler's Christmas Catalogue.

  - *Search Service:* Search services will be offered (free, or at varying costs) for out-of-print books. The search will be in our city or we will advertise nationwide in trade journals to fulfill customers' requests.

  - *The Successful Bookstore's* best and most important service will be the breadth (selection) of stock, and its depth (numbers of copies of important titles).

Breadth/Depth

We will:

- Specialize in specific merchandise categories based upon targeted customers' interests and financial objectives.

- Ensure that our assortment's breadth and depth will be comparable to larger stores in both front and backlist for key categories.

- Ensure that our assortment's breadth will be competitive with superstores in frontlist for selected key categories.

- Carry important frontlist books for customers in all categories.

- Make the best titles available from both small and large presses for targeted customers.

Promotional Program

- *The Successful Bookstore's* presence will be felt in the community it serves by supporting reading related activities both in and outside of our stores, e.g., autographings, book fairs, literary and library events.

PDM (Planning, Design, and Merchandising)

- The plan, design, and merchandising will balance the assortment's size with the customer's need for seating and browsing space.

- The design will be appealing to a female book buyer/mall shopper, whether classified as middle market or upscale.

- The children's department will be sensational, with space for storytelling.

Enticing announcements of in-store events greet customers entering this bookstore. LIBERTIES Fine Books & Music, Boca Raton, Fla.

customer needs for security, comfort, stimulation, and variety. The arrangement of bookstore space, equipment, and amenities relies heavily on design theories.

This essentially concludes the basic Mission Statement. There is, of course, opportunity to expand, reduce, and modify this basic Mission Statement to suit each individual need.

With the basic Mission Statement in hand, our next step is to prepare a competitive positioning and differentiation statement. The purpose of this statement is to compare our proposed store with established booksellers and chain bookstore competition in the general trade area.

Competitive Positioning and Differentiation

One of the touchstones of success lies in the correct positioning and differentiation of our store from established competition.

Assume that *The Successful Bookstore* management has identified a 3,500 - 5,000 square foot space available in a quality upscale regional/strip mall. Let us also assume that there are several malls in the community. We will further assume that two or more of the popular national chain bookstores are established in the city, and that there are one or more successful independents and one or more super bookstores in the trade area.

The objective here is to first define what our new store's competitive position will be and how that position will stack up against competition both now and in the future.

The entrance to this store includes sunlight, a bench, framed testimonials, and access to the customer-service desk. The Black Oak, Berkeley, Calif.

Table 1.9 Competitive Positioning and Differentiation Statement

The Successful Bookstore is planned to be:

- Prototype square footage: 3,500 - 5,000; range of titles: 16,000 - 24,000, with an average of 20,000.

- Designed for the upscale mall shopper/book buyer: "My favorite bookstore because it offers a quality shopping experience."

- Product and service driven in a fashionable setting.

- Lease line emphasis will be generally on "the new and now" while also integrating pertinent local market titles and themes.

- Title mix will be literary but not devoid of "commercial" books.

- Assortments will be focused within specific categories; the mix across categories might appear eclectic but it will be highly congruent with our targeted customer; we will not be a run-of-the-mill supermarket bookstore; we will be a general bookstore with a collection of boutiques - shops within a shop.

- Non-book products will be book related and/or core customer targeted. Non-book products will represent about 12 percent of the store's sales mix; merchandise will be book related non-book items as well as gifts targeted to *The Successful Bookstore's* core customers and used to differentiate it in the market; staffing will be available to support non-book product sales.

- Pricing strategy will be list, supplemented with special value items (e.g., selected remainders and promotional books).

- Prototype will be ambient for the up-market while also being inviting and comfortable for the middle market; it will be especially appealing to women shoppers.

- Focus of the store is on frontlist books and appropriate non-book products; backlist representing the best in our key categories will be stocked.

- Emphasis will be placed on making the store accessible to the elderly and handicapped.

Three levels of open selling can be found in the Academic Bookstore, the largest of its kind in Europe. Academic Bookstore, Helsinki, Finland.

Financial Strategy

To prepare for and plan *The Successful Bookstore's* financial structure and implementation, we must develop a Financial Strategy Statement listing things to be done, items to be prepared, and decisions to be made. At Ken White Associates, we can and do provide a great deal of proven advice to help develop financial strategies for new and remodeled stores.

A good source of background information is a fine book entitled *Operating a Bookstore,* by Elliott Leonard. His chapter on "Financial Factors" deals with budgeting, operating expense control, merchandise cost control or cost of sales, and money handling and usage. It concludes with a review of bookkeeping practices, and is well worth reading.

For now, however, we present in Table 1.10 an outline of what a financial strategy should address. Store location, retail charges, build-out costs, and investment are further discussed in Chapter 2.

Table 1.10   Financial Strategy

1. Develop *The Successful Bookstore's* model pro forma.
   A. Determine what sales levels are necessary to generate our targeted internal rate of return (IRR) given a reasonable range of values for gross capital required to build out the store in its proposed configuration.
      1) The impact on IRR for expected amounts of landlord contributed build-out money.
      2) Occupancy expense for the proposed new store in mall (strip centers or CBD/central shopping areas) locations.
2. Distinguish fixed from variable operating costs so that the impact of sales volume changes on store contribution can be modeled.
3. Identify high potential target locations or markets for the store.
4. Once the above tasks are completed, a list of prioritized locations should be developed. Locations should be grouped by developer/landlord and demographics. Meetings with developer/landlord should be held to identify potential sites, rental, build-out costs, and timing.

ABA's *Abacus Report* is another reliable source of operating costs, data, and ratios. At Ken White Associates, we use a database of information collected from hundreds of projects, the *Abacus Report*, and other special data to process, compile, and produce one-to-five or ten-year pro forma statements, cash flow analyses, and inventory cost estimates for store owners, realtors, lenders, and investors (see Appendix II).

Critical Success Factors

There are several factors critical to the success of *The Successful Bookstore* that we must be aware of. Our statement on this issue might include the critical success factors presented in Table 1.11.

Table 1.11   Critical Success Factors

- A store prototype with the right ambiance to consistently attract our targeted customers while also being sought after by the local estate community for future growth.

- A merchandising strategy that is market and customer directed and is well executed in order to drive sales, win and retain customers, and effectively differentiate us in the markets we serve.

- An array of services provided by excellent people who are supported by superior systems so as to ensure that each customer has a quality shopping experience and believes that he or she has received an excellent value.

A successful front-of-store puzzle promotional theme uses the side of a table in its visual merchandising presentation. The Book Nook, Wyckoff, N.J. Please see Page 164 for other merchandising concepts.

How Bookstores Work

As a rule, independent booksellers buy their new book stock from two sources: publishers and wholesalers. For new booksellers, the decision of which to use is usually based on the availability of credit, the titles needed, discounts offered, and speed of delivering the store opening order.

The American Wholesale Booksellers' Association

Directory and Customer Handbook, published by the American Wholesale Booksellers' Association (AWBA),[3] describes member wholesaler services in detail, listing policies, stock type, contact people, discount schedules, and features of their services.

Good service is the key to good business. And good service - high fill rates, accurate fulfillment of your orders, and fast, damage-free shipping - is what you really need and expect from a book wholesaler.

Customer Service

The key to satisfying customers is having the books they want, when they want them. And that's the same goal book wholesalers strive for in serving you. Let's take a look at just how one quality wholesale book company interacts with independent booksellers. Baker & Taylor[4] - B&T, as it is known in the trade - is one of America's premier wholesale book distributors. B&T has developed a unique package of bookseller services, including the largest title base in stock, rapid order fulfillment, toll-free ordering, an electronic ordering system, microfiche service to accommodate special orders, and bi-weekly and monthly book alerts that cover fascinating and informative merchandising features. (Table 1.12 outlines B&T's discount schedule).

Why Use a Wholesaler?

Wholesalers are able to provide faster service than publishers. They also can offer better prices. Book wholesalers usually offer all books and periodicals to booksellers at a 40% discount for telephone orders, and up to 43% for mail or electronic orders (see Table 1.12). Finally, wholesalers offer operational support to independent booksellers.

Orders for books placed with domestic publishers are filled within two to four weeks. Established book wholesalers stock the books and publications of many publishers.

Order Consolidation

As you might expect, quality wholesalers can consolidate your hot title re-orders, special orders, backlist re-orders, and pre-publication title orders. They can ship all types of books, magazines, maps, calendars, audio/video cassettes, and calendars from major and independent small publishers for delivery the next day or soon thereafter, if the item is in their stock. Thus, a wholesaler allows you to consolidate your orders, maximize your discount, and minimize your handling and freight. One order, one package, and one invoice. Consolidation of orders into one shipment from one source reduces freight charges, while uncontrolled freight and handling charges erode your profit picture.

How Same-Day Order Fulfillment Works

Many wholesalers have toll-free lines, immediate stock verification, electronic ordering systems, knowledgeable personnel, and an array of customer-oriented programs. Place your order by 10:30 A.M. (local time), and B&T Books will ship the same day. Orders to U.S. customers are shipped within 24 hours after they are received. B&T also offers special next-day delivery service to many markets. Shipments to Canadian booksellers are made via BATAPAK®, B&T's exclusive delivery system for Canada.

Quality specialty book and magazine wholesalers such as Diamond and Capital City[5] wholesalers fulfill orders nationally for specialty items, comic books, and periodicals in about the same time span.

Let the Wholesaler's Warehouse Be Your Stockroom

Quality book wholesalers are geared to process orders immediately. This allows you to increase your inventory turn by making the wholesaler your "stockroom." And, a single source can eliminate needless back-order problems and design of back room space.

With 50,000 new titles published each year, independent booksellers cannot possibly stock every book that every one of your customers wants. That is one reason why the strategy to let the wholesaler's warehouse be your stockroom has gained such acceptance. For example, with more than 120,000 titles in their inventory list, B&T Books stock the big books from small presses, the small books from big presses, and all the mid-list titles in between. This awesome book inventory gives you access to any book in print that is available through normal wholesale channels. But it also gives B & T and all other wholesalers fits when new store opening orders are not placed far enough in advance. All titles are not always available from all publishers to the wholesaler. This can create a back-order problem that could largely be eliminated by ordering back list items as far in advance as possible. Two to four weeks does not allow enough time. Think more in terms of six to eight weeks to be on the safe side. Wholesalers often stock books that you may not be aware of (specialized, regional, or small press titles). Ask them what they stock, and they will be happy to tell you.

How To Increase Profit Margins

Electronic ordering can give the small independent bookseller a distinct edge: larger discounts with less stock investment and less complications, as we see in Table 1.12.

The straightforward contextural design of this appealing textbook department makes it comfortable, inviting and accessible. Southern Oregon State College, Ashland, Ore.

How Discounts Work

Major publishers usually offer the following discounts to independent booksellers: one to five copies qualifies for a 30% discount, and discounts up to 50% are offered for orders of 100 or more of a single title. Each publisher will provide the bookseller with a printed schedule of terms, discounts, and policies.

Table 1.12   Baker & Taylor Books

	Electronic Orders	Phone/Fax Mail Orders	
Number Of Units Per Title	10+ Units	25+ Units	10-24 Units
1-4	40%	40%	35%
5-9	41%	41%	35%
10+	42%	42%	35%

Discount Schedule
Total Units/Order Size

Payment Terms: 2% days E.O.M. Net 30 days, E.O.M. Please note: a 1.5% per month service charge will be assessed against past-due accounts and shipments may be withheld. Canadian booksellers may pay in U.S. or Canadian funds.

Simply put, when you electronically order ten titles in quantities of from one to four of each title, you get a 40% discount. If you call, mail, or fax in the order, you would have to order two and a half times as many books to get the same discount. That differential can be important in the way a new store works.

Electronic Ordering Equipment Requirements

To place an order, all you need is an IBM or compatible computer and a Hayes or compatible modem. Key in the ISBN and quantity, and transmit the order to B&T via the toll-free phone line. You will know immediately which titles will be shipped, back-ordered, or cancelled. Your order is processed within 24 hours. This fast through-flow of books and sidelines will affect back room planning. Less reserve stock but more back room space may be required.

B&T Link Module 1 makes placing book, audio, and video orders through your PC simple and efficient. B&T Link Module 2, the title source on CD-ROM, is one of the most accurate and sophisticated bibliographic software programs available. Each month, a new CD-ROM is issued, containing 1.2 million book, audio, and video titles, including in-print, out-of-print, and forthcoming titles. Up to 80,000 price and status changes are made monthly.

B&T Link Module 3 is a weekly inventory diskette that will instantly connect you to your regional B&T Books Service Center, telling you what's in stock and what's on order - no more guessing and waiting!

Microfiche Inventory Listings

Whether you do or do not have a computer, a microfiche reader can promote your service image and improve the way your store works. With weekly, alphabetical

Upscale medical book and health-sciences book depart-
ment. Charlesbank Bookshops & Cafe', Boston, Mass.

title listings of B&T inventory on microfiche at your fingertips, you will be able to supply the special order titles your customers request.

With the microfiche access, you can obtain any book in print that is available through normal wholesale channels. Provision must be made in the planning process to power and accommodate microfiche readers and to allow space for customers to comfortably use them.

Conclusion

Bookselling is a complex business made to look simple. Barging into a new business venture - rushing into the planning of a new store that might consume your life savings or corporate budget without carefully and deliberately preparing yourself - is a risky business.

That's why we had to cover this mileage of nitty-gritty, bottom line material before the good stuff.

Now, let's move on.

BOOKSTORE TYPES, LOCATION, AND INVESTMENT CONSIDERATIONS

To decide on the kind of store to open, we must consider not only the targeted market needs but also the kind of bookstore we will enjoy owning. Many kinds of general and specialty bookstores exist to fill every book buyer's needs. The small, general, independent bookstore can range from 200 to 4,000 square feet. The most popular general bookstores are 2,500 to 3,000 square feet, positioned in high-traffic locations, often strip centers and malls. They typically stock 15,000 to 18,000 titles. Most superstores are also general bookstores, often 8,000 to 80,000 square feet in size, with 100,000 to 400,000 books on hand. Related sidelines are offered to broaden their market appeal. Examples of the plans of some of these phenomenal stores are found later in this and in Chapter 4. They are included for general information and to provide you with a broader base of industry information.

General Bookstores

Successful general bookstores characteristically strive to fit in with their market, accumulating a selection of mainstream books and appropriate sidelines customized for family and neighborhood friends and book buyers who enjoy reading for the fun and love of it. General bookstores are also designed to appeal to serious readers with a literary bent as well as customers with specialized professional/technical interests. General bookstores are the backbone of independent bookselling.

Specialty Bookstores and Departments

The term *specialty bookstore* can apply equally to both small and large businesses. Specialty bookstores, as well as specialty departments in large stores, focus on a niche marketing strategy. The store's inventory, image, and promotions are targeted towards a specific segment of customers with an expressed interest in a particular category of books.

Blue and white color ambiance establishes a modern and efficient feeling and pleasant shopping experience in this well merchandised and fixtured bookstore. Pacific Stars & Stripes Bookstore, Yokosuko, Japan.

Specialty bookstores focus their energies on promotional image, inventory, and service in one or more special categories. In large markets, specialty bookstores often concentrate on promoting a distinct category of books relating to technical subjects, law, medicine, dance, ballet, children, travel, etc.

Specialty booksellers are generally better positioned than chain booksellers to know their customers' needs. Specialty independent booksellers round out their merchandise mix with unique sideline items that complement their selection of books, while chain bookstores have a great deal of trouble managing sidelines on a large scale.

Specialty bookstores have long been established and are prevalent throughout the bookselling industry worldwide. Many large bookstores have successfully developed specialty book departments. Deciding which department to specialize in is based on analysis of prior purchase records (credit card charge slips) and current sales analysis provided by in-store POS, or point-of-sale, terminals (see Glossary).

The Many Kinds of Specialty Bookstores

There are many types of specialty bookstores. Each type offers opportunity to the open-minded, imaginative, and resourceful bookseller.

The Anne Hughes Coffee Room is a customer convenience welcomed by the staff and shoppers. Powell's City of Books, Portland, Ore.

Table 2.1	A Partial Listing of Popular Types of Specialty Bookstores
Visitor Information Bookshops	Christian Bookstores
Museum Shops	Judaic Bookstores
Cafe Bookshops	New Age, Metaphysical,
Book-and-Coffee Roasting Shops	Feminist, Gay/Lesbian
The Business & Law Bookshop	Bookstores
Mystery Bookshops	Dance Bookstores
Poetry Bookshops	"How To" Bookstores
Ballet Bookstores	Maritime Bookstores
Technical Bookstores	Nature Bookshops
Art Bookshops	The Travel Bookshop
Children's Bookshops	The Drama Bookshop
Law/Medical Bookshops	Comic Book Stores
The Second-Hand Bookstore	The Cook Bookshop
Periodical Bookstores	Biography Bookstores
Technical and Computer Bookstores	Medical Bookstores

Specialty bookshops are popular in cities and markets where there are groups of people interested in these specialty subjects. Locating a specialized bookshop convenient to readers of its specialty category is advisable. It should also be positioned in a location with the population base to support the particular specialty bookstore business one has in mind to allow it to thrive.

Superstores

There are five identifiable classes of superstores today. First are large, established independent bookstores: Powell's City of Books, Portland, Oregon; The Tattered Cover, Denver, Colorado; Cody's, Berkeley, California; and Taylors, Dallas, Texas. All are well over 15,000 square feet in size. These stores have been in business for a long time and have provided a prototype for the chain superstores that now

Fiction and literature section of a general independent bookstore. Webster's Books, Lansing, Mich.

follow. Many independent superstores provide cafes and coffee bars as customer conveniences.

The second class of superstores includes the major university bookstores with large general book and reference departments. The Charlesbank Bookshops & Cafe' at Boston University, University Bookstores in Madison, Wisconsin, The Co-op at the University of Washington, Seattle, and the Harvard Co-op in Boston are all stores that have provided quality service on a very large scale for a very long time. Some of these stores also provide cafes and coffee bars.

The third group of superstores are local and regional independent bookseller chains: Kroch's and Brentano's (Chicago), Hunters (Dallas), Webster's Books (Lansing and Ann Arbor, Michigan), and the Davis Kidd Stores in Tennessee.

Fourth are the free-standing independent superstores. *LIBERTIES* (Boca Raton, Florida) and Bollinger Books in Oklahoma City each have a unique image, with cafes and espresso bars. And finally, there are the new chain superstores.

Chain Superstores

As we see in the accompanying examples of their layouts, there is considerable variation among superstores in the Barnes & Noble group: more "plain Jane" types of stores are being built than the glamorous style portrayed in most press releases. The elegant stores found in Paramus, New Jersey and New York City, New York, are nowhere to be seen in Lansing, Michigan or Burlington, Vermont. There, one is struck by the obvious "slimmed down" version, which is devoid of many of the chain's usual features, facilities, and services to reduce construction and start-up costs. Among stores in this chain, it appears that only the name and policies are the same.

There is, at present, visible market segmentation among the major chain superstores, with Barnes & Noble Bookstores, Bookstop, Bookstar, and Crown Books, among others, adapting what appears to be a "Toys R' Us" approach to site location, layout, and merchandising. A mass quantity discount statement is made at the front, and an overwhelming number of gondolas are placed at right angles to the flow of traffic. Four to ten cashiers are typically found in the layout, with a counting room, two offices, and a large back room in support of the operation.

Most Borders Book Shops, recently acquired by Kmart, are well located and positioned for the long haul. Generally devoid of distinctive interior atmosphere, the Borders Book Shops built to date are large, well lighted, and clean. Newer stores include an espresso/coffee bar. It is believed by many that the initial success of the Borders Book Shops triggered the movement of the major book chains into the superstore business.

Waldenbooks, a division of Kmart's new Basset Book Shops, has also entered the scene. The prototype store gave the impression of one conceived and implemented by a committee. It seemed to miss the mark on both merchandising and design levels. But those deficiencies will work themselves out as this new group of stores matures and finds its niche among other national chain bookstore competitors.

Floor Plans

The newer Super Crown Bookstores recently built on the west coast are apparently successful. But they appear to be heavily committed to paper-bound editions, with a strong discount remainder book statement at the front, supported by deep-discount *New York Times* bestsellers and magazines. Described by some as glitzy, with an excess of gold trim and plastic crowns resembling old refrigerator logos, the stores do meet a market need and deliver a range of goods and services.

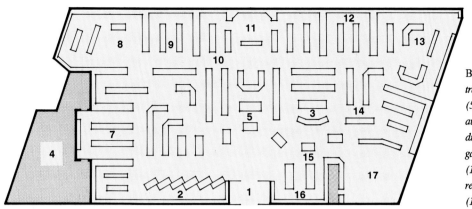

Basset Book Shop - Superstore, Stanford, Conn. *(1) Entrance; (2) cashiers; (3) service desk; (4) offices/back room; (5) NYT hardcover bestsellers; (6) bargain books; (7) audio, fiction & literature, mystery, science fiction; (8) children's; (9) health, psychology; (10) sports, travel, hobbies, games; (11) art, home, cooking; (12) business, computers; (13) science & nature, reference; (14) history, biography, religion, social science; (15) new releases; (16) magazines; (17) coffee bar.*

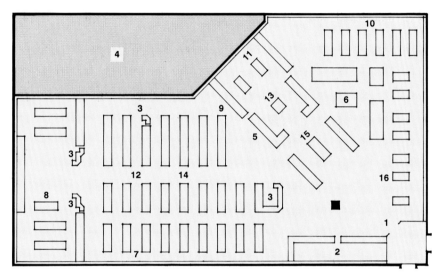

Barnes & Noble (Small) Superstore, Danbury, Conn. *(1) Entrance; (2) cashiers; (3) service desk; (4) offices/back room; (5) NYT hardcover bestsellers; (6) bargain books; (7) audio, fiction & literature, mystery, science fiction; (8) children's; (9) health, psychology; (10) sports, travel, hobbies, games; (11) art, home, cooking; (12) business, computers; (13) science & nature, reference; (14) history, biography, religion, social science; (15) new releases; (16) magazines.*

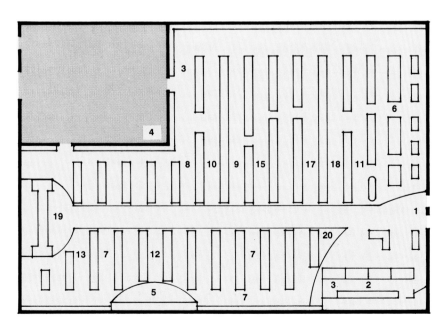

BOOKSTAR Superstore, Torrance, Calif. *(1) Entrance; (2) cashiers; (3) service desk; (4) offices/back room; (5) NYT hardcover bestsellers; (6) bargain books; (7) fiction & literature, mystery, science fiction; (8) children's; (9) health; (10) sports; (11) art; (12) computers; (13) science & nature; (14) reference; (15) history; (16) biography; (17) religion; (18) magazines; (19) adventure & spy.*

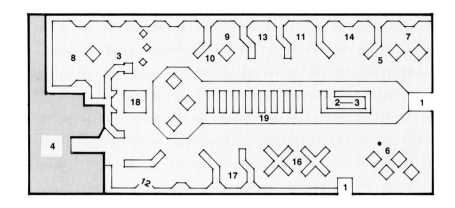

Little Professor, Prototype Bookstore, Ann Arbor, Mich. *(1) Entrance; (2) cashiers; (3) service desk; (4) offices/back room; (5) NYT hardcover bestsellers; (6) bargain books; (7) audio, fiction & literature, mystery, science fiction; (8) children's; (9) health, psychology; (10) sports, travel, hobbies, games; (11) art, home, cooking; (12) business, computers; (13) science & nature, reference; (14) history, biography, religion, social science; (15) new releases; (16) magazines; (17) true crime, new age, philosophy, recovery; (18) fireplace/signings; (19) paper-bound fiction.*

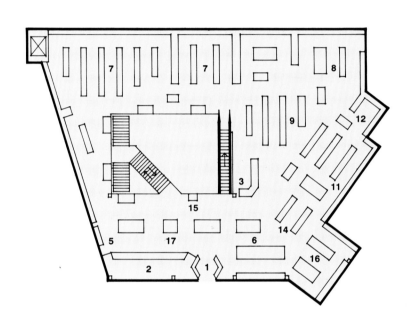

Borders Book Shop, Pittsburgh, Pa., Upstairs. *(1) Entrance; (2) cashiers; (3) service desk; (4) offices/back room; (5) NYT hardcover bestsellers; (6) sale books; (7) fiction and literature, mystery, science fiction; (8) health, psychology; (9) travel, maps; (10) cooking and nutrition; (11) business, computers; (12) science; (13) greeting cards; (14) books on tape; (15) staff selection; (16) magazines, newspapers; (17) new fiction and non-fiction.*

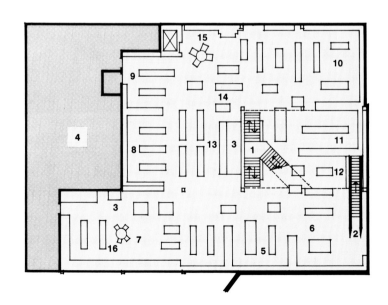

Borders Book Shop, Pittsburgh, Pa., Downstairs. *(1) Stairs; (2) escalator; (3) service desk; (4) offices/back room; (5) architecture & design; (6) art & photography; (7) children; (8) family & parenting, social science, psychology, self help; (9) philosophy; (10) history & political science; (11) reference; (12) music, media, film, posters, blank books, journals; (13) humor & games; (14) plants, animals, nature, gardening; (15) fireplace; (16) reading/signing area.*

A unique specialty travel bookstore. ABOVE: Lighted globe display. CENTER: Travel accessories and guides. BELOW: Folded maps and guides.
Powell's Travel Bookstore, Portland, Ore.

Popular Book Category Lists, Sidelines, and Store Services

Think of the category list as a menu of books and periodicals that customers need and want to buy. In many respects, imaginative category lists can help set the tone and image of the store. Remember, there is nothing fixed or rigid about these lists. We can change them and change them again. One of your most important jobs will be to develop the category list for your new store (see Appendix II).

Each bookstore has a personality and stock of books all its own, arranged by category. The better you mesh your own list of titles and categories to the demographics of the market, the more likely you are to succeed. In addition to the sample General Bookstore Key Category list in Chapter 1, sample category lists and directories of services and sidelines are provided in Tables 2.2 and 2.3 to give you a better idea of what these important lists are and how they are organized.

Travel Bookstores

A specialty store devoted exclusively to books, guides, and maps on local and world travel may include many out-of-print, rare, and hard-to-find titles as well as a comprehensive selection of foreign language dictionaries and travel videos.

Table 2.2   Travel Bookstore Category, Sideline, and Service List

Main Sections:

Travel - U.S.	World & Foreign Travel
Travel - Canada	Travel Essays
Travel - Europe	Regional Travel
Travel - Asia/Africa	Foreign Language
Travel - Caribbean	Dictionaries
Travel - Australia/Pacific	Atlases
Books on local arts, customs, and food	Road Atlases
	Rolled and Folded Maps
Hiking Guides	City Guides

Foreign Travel Guides and Maps: Baedeker, Faber, David and Charles, Nagel's, Fursts, Hallwag maps, Benn Blue guides, Falk Plan, Kummerly & Frey, Bartholomew, Bali maps, Michelin guides to all countries in the world.

Sidelines: Espresso/coffee bar, travel videos, audio tapes, globes, travel accessories, pay telephones, bookmarks.

Services: International mail order, special order, search service, travel agency, travel insurance, credit cards.

The Cook Bookshop

The most impressive specialty establishments are modern, well lit, floored with large ceramic tiles, and comprehensive in their range, with some three- to five-thousand titles on cooking in stock: everything from apple strudel in Vienna to Po' Boys in New Orleans!

Some fascinating shops incorporate, at the back, a demonstration cooking area below a glass roof. Others offer coffee, cake, and lunch cooked from recipes out of new books. Others offer private conference dining rooms (usually upstairs) served by a separate pantry-kitchen. Themes vary from California texture (wine and cheese) to New York chic (Quiche Lorraine).

Table 2.3   Cook Bookstore Category, Sidelines, and Service   List
(1,500 to 2,000 square feet)

Main Sections:

Cookbooks	Wine & Spirits
Entertaining	Herbs
Frugal Gourmet	Fruits & Vegetables
Seafood	Barbecue
Bread & Muffins	Salad/Desserts
Professional Cooking	Culinary Essays
James Beard/Craig Claiborne	Special Diets
Vegetarian	International Cooking:
Diet/Nutrition	Mexican, Indian,
Weight Control	Italian, Jewish,
Health/Fitness	Cajun, Oriental
Calories & Cholesterol	Healthy Cooking
Cookbooks on Cassettes	

Sidelines: Related periodicals, second-hand cookbooks in mint condition, remainders, bookmarks, gadgets.

Services: Mail order, special orders, cooking demonstrations, buy second-hand books, credit cards.

Assuming that you are still convinced that opening a new bookstore is the right thing to do, and you know the kind of bookstore you want to open and operate, the next step is to find the ideal location.

Location, Location, Location

No decision is more important than selecting the right location for business. Even if you have ample financial resources and above-average managerial skills, they cannot offset the handicap of a poor location. Many retailers select a store site by chance, but the best stores are the result of taking the time to check every option rather than plunging blindly ahead without proper guidance and understanding. The life of many new stores begins with a Site Evaluation Study.

Site Evaluation Studies

A site evaluation study is an evaluation of the feasibility of a given location for the type of store we plan to open. Today, site evaluation studies follow a streamlined research and analysis process designed to arrive at a carefully reasoned recommendation.

Site and Market Analysis

Signing a lease that commits you to ten or more years of rent payments involves substantial risk. Even for a bookstore with several units, one non-performing location can create negative cash flow for the whole business. Therefore, it's critical that emerging booksellers select locations and negotiate lease terms with care.

One way of increasing the odds for success is to use the services of a retail consultant. At Ken White Associates, Site and Market Analysis services supplement ABA Site Location Services (see Appendix II).

Demographic reports, as discussed in Chapter 1, tell us who lives where and the dollar value of the target market. Finding the right store location in your market to take advantage of the opportunity is an entirely different matter.

Statistics do not tell everything. The character of the location, its affordability, the rental offer, CAM (common area maintenance) costs, quality of landlord management and center maintenance, strength of the retail market, landlord vs. tenant expectations, and the reasonableness of the Tenant Criteria and Requirements (see Appendix I) demanded by the landlord are serious issues to understand, weigh, and decide on to round out the scenario.

Character and Site Location

The character, location, image, and appearance of both the store and neighborhood must appeal to the kind of customers we wish to attract. There are almost as many distinct types of locations as there are different kinds of bookstores. Bookstores are located at street level, in basements, on second and upper floors, in strip center malls, and in freestanding houses, retail stores, restaurants, theaters, supermarkets, and furniture and appliance stores, to name just a few. Their various appeals may be greatly enhanced or diminished by the size of the market, their location in the community, and their general appearance.

Site Location Factors

Booksellers searching out a new location should look into affordability of space, area demographics, and center management. Your key to finding the best location for your bookstore is to closely examine the following issues:

1. *Demographics.* Prior to center construction, every professional developer will prepare a marketing study and update it yearly. It is important to examine the studies to learn as much as possible about the target area. Data provided by

most malls, landlords, and Chambers of Commerce will describe the community's demographics.

2. *The Local Retail Environment.* The strip center location, rental costs, marketing and advertising plan, and management all influence the correct rental decision. You must first consider the strength of the retail environment by asking existing tenants what they like and dislike about the strip center. By visiting the site on Saturday and again on Tuesday morning, a bookseller can see firsthand the different levels of traffic at the site.

3. *Affordability.* Finding the most affordable address for your business is important. You should compare the cost of rent for strip center space against regional small space in your area with the Urban Land Institute's *Dollars and Cents of Shopping Centers*, available in your local library.

4. *Center Promotion Plan.* If you decide on a strip or mall center, look for a promotional plan that includes marketing and advertising services. Is the following provided?

   • A marketing plan with scheduled special promotional activities that allow the mall manager and tenants to interact and share experiences.

   • Advertising opportunities for both the individual tenant and the center, to raise community awareness and interest.

   • Additional assistance from outside merchandising consultants regarding display goods, sales incentives, and overall tenant performance.

5. *Quality and Appearance of Mall Management.* The appearance of the strip center plays a big role in the quality of management. If signs are left unlit, parking lots are full of pot holes, landscaping is not maintained, and garbage is not emptied regularly, that will no doubt indicate that something is wrong with the management.

   If the site is half-full, you need to find out why. The manager may have upgraded the mall and raised the rent, or tenants may have moved. You should also investigate the success rate of the existing tenants by looking at sales-tax figures from the marketing study.

Table 2.4 Estimated Investment for a New Independent Bookstore (1,500 to 4,000 square feet)			
Type Of Expense	**Estimated Amount/Range**		
	Low	Median	High
Leasehold Improvement	4,900	7,000	11,000
Fixtures and Equipment	34,900	55,000	65,000
Initial Inventory	$50,500	$66,000	$132,000
Total Capital Investment			
Grand Opening Promotions	1,500	3,000	4,000
Working Capital	15,000	25,000	35,000
Miscellaneous	5,000	7,000	9,000
Total Initial Investment	$111,800	$163,000	$256,000

6. *Future Center Plans.* Find out when the center was last renovated or if there are any plans to renovate in the future. If you rent before renovation, you may not incur the costs of the upgrade.

7. *Landlord Relationships.* Know what you can expect from the landlord and what the landlord expects from you. All larger shopping malls provide prospective tenants with a statement of Tenant Criteria and Requirements.

A sample Tenant Criteria and Requirements document is found in Appendix I. Aside from stipulating the scope of work to be provided by the tenant, these documents contain valuable technical information that can be relied upon for the designing of quality bookstores. You will find answers to lots of sticky questions here.

Remember: landlords can be good guys too. They need good, reliable tenants and the comfort of knowing that they will have a steady income in future years.

Money

What will it cost to open a bookstore? A guide to determine current estimates of the amount of your initial investment to open one of several types and sizes of independent bookstores follows in Table 2.4 and Table 2.5 The amounts shown are our best current estimates of what new booksellers will typically need to spend for the purposes indicated. The actual costs incurred by a particular situation may be higher or lower, depending on the particular circumstances of the store and the bookseller.

Factors Affecting Initial Investment

The actual initial investment is influenced by the type of location selected (strip shopping center, enclosed mall, or free-standing site); whether the site has existing improvements that we can use; the amount, if any, of the landlord's allowance for leasehold improvements; size and location of the site; the region in which the store is located; discretionary expenditures of the bookseller; the availability of leasing or financing arrangements for certain items; and the bookseller's credit rating.

Table 2.5 Estimated Investment for a Superstore (10,000 to 25,000 square feet)			
Type Of Expense	**Estimated Amount/Range**		
	Low	Median	High
Leasehold Improvement	215,000	365,000	425,000
Fixtures and Equipment	125,000	200,000	275,000
Initial Inventory	400,000	750,000	1,000,000
Total Capital Investment	$740,000	$1,315,000	$1,700,000
Grand Opening Promotions	15,000	15,000	35,000
Working Capital	75,000	100,000	150,000
Miscellaneous	10,000	20,000	35,000
Total Initial Investment	$840,000	$1,490,000	$1,920,000

Larger stores cost proportionally more than small stores in some categories and less in others. That is because certain basic costs, common to all stores, can be amortized over a larger area and generally for a longer period of time, as we see in Table 2.5.

Assumptions

The estimates assume that you are leasing space as opposed to purchasing land and/or a building for the development of the store. The amounts estimated for working capital assume that you will have other funds or income (from a source other than your store) to cover your living expenses for at least 18 months after you open the new store.

The Plain Vanilla Box

The lease for a bookstore in a new strip shopping center typically provides the bookseller with a "vanilla box" consisting of sheetrock finished walls between neighboring tenants, a standardized store front, HVAC (heating, ventilation, and air conditioning), a rest room, and basic lighting and electrical outlets conforming to code.

Leasehold Improvements

For a small specialty and medium-sized general bookstore, the leasehold improvements expense estimate covers the installation of fixtures, carpeting, painting, sprinklers, the installation of partition walls to separate the stock room from the sales areas, and basic electrical work, including the installation of the telephone and computer cable. The Tenant Criteria and Requirements (see Appendix I) describe the scale and quality of improvements you will be expected to provide, and a description of the landlord's participation.

Build-Out Allowances

The landlord may agree to provide the bookstore owner with a build-out allowance to cover all or part of the cost of the leasehold improvements, which will reduce the initial investment you must make while decreasing your monthly rent expense. We expect that in most cases, landlords will agree to provide an owner with a build-out allowance to cover all or part of the costs of the leasehold improvements.

Negotiating Build-Out Allowances

During the past few years, we have been able to negotiate build-out and fixturing allowances from the landlords of superstores which range in total value from $30 per square foot of leased area to the total cost of build-out, store fixtures, fees, computer systems, and graphics. Remember: you must negotiate with the landlord to provide a build-out allowance to cover all or part of the leasehold improvements before you sign a lease.

Cost of Store Fixtures and Equipment

The fixture and equipment expense covers book and magazine display fixtures, the customer service area, a computerized retail operating system including point-of-sale terminals, allowances for in-bound freight, the outfitting of a basic office in the back room area, exterior, and interior signage and graphics.

Two-level specialty art and poster shop.
Blackwell's Art & Poster Shop, Oxford, U.K.

POS and Inventory Control Systems

The retail operating system for a new, independent super-bookstore requires more point-of-sale terminals than a small specialty shop. Customarily, four point-of-sale terminals at the customer service counter (to manage inventory, make book title searches, and cash out) plus one to two additional terminals for customer assistance, one terminal for the back room, and one in the office for management and fiscal control are required.

Superstore Improvement Expense

For a superstore, the leasehold improvements expense covers the installation of fixtures, floor and wall coverings, electrical work, and other expenses of improving the space as necessary to meet the building requirements and PDM specifications of the tenant bookstore.

Grand Opening Promotion

A grand opening promotion is essential to establish the new store in the community. Planning for the grand opening is begun during initial Mission Statement development.

Working Capital

Individual needs for working capital may vary considerably. As a rule of thumb, set aside a minimum of six months' rent.

Miscellaneous

Miscellaneous expenses include the cost of attending the ABA Booksellers' School, pre-paid deposits, and pre-paid expenses such as store bags, store supplies, and insurance.

Initial Inventory

The initial inventory required for a new independent bookstore varies with the size of the store. It features a product mix of books, magazines, and book-related sidelines, including trade books (90% of the total inventory investment), magazines, books-on-tape (audio cassettes), inexpensive classical music tapes, children's learning materials, bookmarks, and book plates.

Storefront, antiquarian book deprtment.
Moe's, Berkeley, Calif.

Estimation of Amount of Stock

You can calculate the number of volumes in your average stock if you figure $5 as the average cost-price of a book to be stocked in a new up-market bookstore. Extra or reserve stock is included in these figures, but its proportion to stock for shelves and display will vary according to the shop's geographic location.

The number of books stocked in the store will vary with the category, class of book, mass-market quality paper, hardbound, over-sized, etc. On the average, ten books to a foot can be used to estimate the quantity of stock for shelves. Table capacity is more variable and must be estimated according to the number of shelves underneath and the kind of display used on top.

Some stores far away from publishing and wholesale shipping centers (Alaska, the Caribbean, and the Far East, for example) will naturally have to carry a greater reserve than those with access to quick deliveries. Every store, moreover, will need more than its average stock during Christmas and other rush seasons.

CHAPTER 3

PLANNING, DESIGN, AND MERCHANDISING SPECIFICATIONS

Before we can actually design a bookstore for you, we must anticipate how the store will function in the space available. Together we must decide on your present and future needs, activities, equipment, special allocations, and other particulars. Your ideas, plans, goals, and objectives must be gathered in a systematic manner to establish a plan of action. We refer to this plan of action as a *PDM Spec*, short for Planning, Design, and Merchandising Specifications.

PDM Spec

The PDM Spec generally takes the form of a written document in which background information, analysis of facts, evaluation, goals, and conclusions relevant to the particular bookstore are documented and presented in a clear, organized manner. The PDM Spec is used to facilitate communication between the KWA design team and you, our client team. The PDM Spec establishes the basic goals and objectives for our joint use during and after the concept development, planning and design phase.

For large projects, it is usually a good idea to have all team members involved from the beginning. Once it is completed, all team members should review the PDM Spec. We find it worthwhile to then conduct a day-long internal briefing session to bring the entire team up to speed on the status of the project, retail themes, and project constraints before actual planning begins. The PDM process begins with data collection.

Data Collection

We collect and categorize only information and facts that are pertinent to the PDM goals of a specific project. A PDM Spec must include descriptions of user characteristics, economic data, and statistical facts. Also included might be local, state, and federal ADA regulations concerning restrictions and zoning, and health,

The simplicity of the interior architecture emphasizes in-store visual merchandising. Natural colors provide a soft, non-distracting background for bookselling. Galleria Bookstore, Atlanta, Ga.

safety, fire, and building codes. Other information included in the PDM Spec is based more on numerical data, such as the pro forma sales plan, title capacity, estimates, schedules, and size of staff. After collecting the necessary data, we use **it as a basis for further planning. The data collected is organized into a document that summarizes the goals of the project and the issues to be addressed.** We discuss these objectives and issues extensively with you prior to the commencement of planning. We make sure that we are all in consensus with the direction of concept development and planning. A key point in the development of the PDM Spec is an understanding of the organization of your new store.

Organization Goals

Bookstores should be organized to meet the needs of the customer, from imminent buying, routine purchases, and major book purchases to social shopping. To meet these needs most efficiently, a bookstore is divided into front and back. A design atmosphere with customer appeal is created in the front sales area. Book processing, services, and management occupy the back room. In some situations, the two overlap, or are at least exposed to one another.

Tasteful exterior. Community Bookstore, Brooklyn, N.Y.

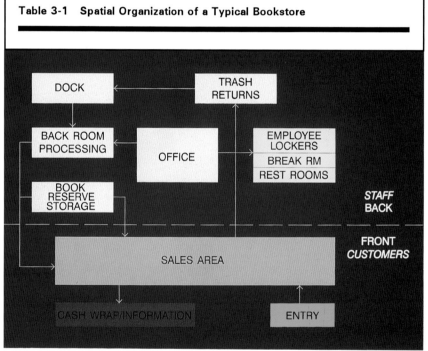

Table 3-1   Spatial Organization of a Typical Bookstore

Atmosphere

How does one develop the PDM Spec for creating an atmosphere in a bookstore? One way is to program the design coordinate of everything from the style of lettering on the facade to the store bags. We would begin by asking: Do you plan to attract an upmarket Galleria clientele, or a funky Greenwich Village literary crowd? Are you going to be selling books to people in a suburban town who are keen on mysteries? Or will you be providing educational books and supplies for a medical school in Boston? Are you thinking of a brilliantly lit discount bookstore, a mass

Large, interior mall storefront - based on an English shop design - is made of red oak. Galleria Bookstore, Atlanta, Ga.

market store, or a used-book shop? Are you planning to have storytelling sessions or open cooking demonstrations or in-store entertainment? And, finally, where do you plan to open this bookstore? Among semitropical Floridian plant life? On a red-brick state university campus? In the slick, sassy surroundings of Chicago's near north side? Only by answering these and similar questions will you begin heading in the right direction to specify and program the proper atmosphere for your new store.

Programming the Storefront

The first impression of a bookstore front may form from a passing glimpse as a shopper drives by in an automobile or rides by in a bus. Or it may form from a closer view while a shopper is walking along a mall or sidewalk.

A typical pedestrian takes less than 7 seconds to pass an average show window. Fast-moving motor traffic takes only 3 seconds. For your bookstore to be successful, every principle that will focus and hold attention to the storefront must be put to work. It will take all that we or any professional can offer to equal the average stopping power of most show windows - less than 10 percent of all sidewalk traffic - and to pass the top mark of 20 percent set by better-than-average displays. Intelligent, professional PDM Spec planning is vital to ensure that the visual appeal of signs and displays produces effective pull-in power.

Tasteful, easily read overhead signs and a general impression of colorful merchandise in the show window usually will be enough to attract fast-moving customer traffic. There must be room enough along the storefront for comfortable window shopping conditions, as well as an easy transition between the storefront displays and interior sales space. The front entrance must always be designed for moving crowds.

Programming Storefront Materials

The doors, glass, lighting, and materials used in storefront construction should clearly express the character of the store. For example, one would choose very different facing materials, sign lettering, and show-window height and arrangements for children's stores than for mystery shops and general superstores.

ABOVE: Brilliantly lit interior becomes part of the storefront in this contextural design concept for an interior mall bookstore. Kroch's & Brentano's, Watertower Place, Chicago, Ill. *CENTER: Exterior traditional red oak entrance doors are accented by a park-bench green storefront with lighted welcome sign in the transom.* Webster's Books, Ann Arbor, Mich. *BELOW: Handsome storefront design adapted to street-front exterior location, modeled in a traditional theme with painted gold lettering.* Book-Friends Cafe', New York City.

ABOVE: Traditional interior English shopfront with security controls. Graphics are applied, moulded Roman lettering. Concept is based on design by Thomas King, London, 1834. Charlesbank Bookshops & Cafe', Boston, Mass. CENTER: Electrically operated interior storefront closure grille designed for free passage of large numbers of people. University Bookstore, Madison, Wis. BELOW: New freestanding bookstore building was programmed with two levels of sales and administrative space. Biola University Bookstore, La Mirada, Calif.

Awnings, which are popular with many bookstores, are appropriate for most types of bookstores and in most locations.

Exterior storefronts exposed to the elements require sturdy material that is impervious to weather. Storefronts located in interior spaces must also be sturdy and sound in construction. Interior storefronts can take advantage of design techniques and materials (such as plastic laminate, open-joint glazing, and roll-up grille doors) that are not practical in exterior storefront construction.

Storefront lighting should be simple and inexpensive to operate. Window lighting can be controlled by manual switches or by time or solenoid switches, which automatically turn the lights on when it becomes dark outside.

Programming the Interior Entry Space

The entryway of the store should motivate the customer to come in and begin browsing. The entry and cash wrap areas frequently give a glimpse of the sales area spaces and experiences that lie within. In some cases, entries are designed to be comfortable environments themselves; in other situations, entry areas lead directly to the selling space.

Programming Sales Space

Sales spaces should be visually oriented to cash wraps and information centers, inward to a focal point, or compartmentalized into particular category departments.

Customer circulation paths through the sales space are defined according to targeted buying habits. Some circulation paths are designed for quick or impulse purchases. Other layouts may entice a buyer to move more slowly and be introduced to highlighted merchandise. For all sales space layouts, it is essential to have good visual control of merchandise and signage for merchandising, customer comfort, customer service, and security.

Programming Flex Space

Flexible, or flex, space is often provided for in both small and large stores. Most often, flex space occurs between the sales and cash wrap areas. This space is intended to provide proper separation between the sales and service fixtures of the store and to accommodate additional stock as needed. Interior flex space can be used to heighten customers' anticipation as they move from one category section of the store to another. Flex space between the back room and the sales area should be programmed to accommodate floor bulk stock at Christmas and other busy times.

Programming Store Fixtures

In the PDM Spec phase, fixture selection is generic. For example, the proposed storytelling feature of our children's department may need individual seating and a table surface for eight little people. We do not determine at this point whether the table is to be round, square, or oblong. Seating is specified only as to the number of individual chairs; style and materials are selected later.

Where there is a need for a special type of fixture (such as an information or service desk to hold a certain type of computer, its printer, modem, and other related equipment) the specifics should be noted early on. If existing fixtures are to be incorporated into a new design, especially if the pieces are unique, these specifics also should be noted in the early PDM Spec stage. In the case of fixture reuse, the PDM Spec should document all requirements through an existing-fixture survey. The survey should list the function, size, color, condition, and other special features of particular store fixtures.

Individual computer demonstration stations in specialty computer bookstore. NYU Book Center, New York City.

Programming, Cash Handling, and Accounting Facilities

The PDM Spec should address the multitude of financial transactions and services that the store will provide. The daily routine of bookstore operations and customer relations dictates the functional layout, acoustical control, and lighting of spaces.

Cash, check, and credit card handling equipment, terminals and cash registers, safes, cash bags, and related equipment are needed in bookstores of all sizes. Large stores often require counting rooms, fitted with alarm devices, for electronic money-counting and auditing machines. Separate facilities to accommodate services for accounts receivable and payable may also be required. With the prevailing trend to longer store hours, cash substations, or drop safes, can be built into cash wrap stations and programmed to provide change during off hours.

Programming Work Centers

At the heart of every large bookstore business office is the all-purpose area designated as the work center or workroom. Typically, workrooms are programmed to be closed off, because they are generally cluttered and filled with noisy equipment, such as printers, copiers, and mailing machines. Work centers can be programmed to contain the central files, paper, and other office equipment supplies, and to provide a general work space for activities such as mailings. In smaller stores, the workroom doubles as the employee break area.

Programming Staff Amenities

Space is often programmed to provide special areas for staff that may not seem directly related to their jobs but are crucial for their well-being. Space for socializing and an escape from the daily routine are provided in a lunch/coffee-break space and similar areas. Other amenities may include staff rest rooms, drinking fountains, lockers, and vending areas. All of these are important ingredients for developing a contented staff: they increase employee satisfaction and productivity.

Public, handicapped-accessible rest rooms must comply with ADA requirements. This quality store is also provided with baby-changing stations and a drinking fountain. UBS Kids, Madison, Wis. Please see Pages 94, 95.

Rest Rooms, Baby-Changing Stations, and Service Closets

Rest rooms for new and renovated bookstores must comply with ADA guidelines, which are now incorporated into most municipal building codes. Grab-bars, impervious surfacing material, and clear space for maneuvering wheel chairs in public rest rooms are mandatory. Lavatory height is specified, and self-closing water valves that remain open for at least 10 seconds are also required. Electrically powered, flashing fire alarms that function as visual emergency alarms in conjunction with audible alarm devices are mandatory in many cities.

Fold-down baby-changing stations are provided in many new children's bookstores and general superstores. This is an amenity appreciated by many young mothers and fathers.

A service closet should be installed in the same vicinity as these utility spaces. The service closet should include a service sink, hot water heater, supply shelves, and space for storing vacuum cleaners, supplies, mops, and a stepladder.

Communication Analysis

The PDM Spec must address the electronic and communication requirements of the store. Bookstores of the 1990s are highly computerized and many of their transactions are electronic. Most stores are provided with ample telephones, as well as credit card approval and cash stations. Telefax machines are found in more and more bookstores. Data is fed from POS terminals into a store's PC or mainframe computer, which may be in the same store or at a remote main store. There are also sophisticated ROM-CDs, CRTs, and modems to be provided for. One of the main design concerns of a bookstore that the PDM should address, the security and monitoring of inventory controls, financial transactions, order processing, and returns, will be discussed in Chapter 9.

Programming Floor Covering

The floor is one of the most important design elements in a bookstore. The PDM Floor Spec should reflect what will be the overall image of the store. Is it fun and funky? Does it impart a relaxed, casual feeling? Or is it elegant and refined? What types of flooring will reflect the store's image? How will the flooring material relate to the rest of the palette of materials? Once the imagery is programmed and established and the division of space is defined, a careful analysis of flooring options is in order.

Carpet Characteristics. Carpet is one of the most popular retail flooring finishes, partly because it is easiest to walk on and softens noise levels, but also because it is relatively inexpensive, easy to install, and easy to maintain. Contract carpet used in most bookstores must pass a Class B flame-spread rating of 75 or less to comply with prevailing fire codes. Usually, three piles of yarn are constructed into tufted level-loop and cut-pile carpet, layered with a polypropylene primary backing, and to this, a second, jute backing is adhered. Carpet is normally manufactured in 12-foot widths, with the largest rolls averaging about 100 linear feet. Carpet and carpet edges must comply with ADA specifications.

Wood Flooring. Wood flooring is often programmed in bookstores because of its durability and ambiance. Wood flooring brings a comfortable warmth and richness to a bookstore. Parquet tiles, inlaid borders, and a multitude of slat and plank designs are readily available. Prefinished wood materials are quickly and easily installed. Unfinished wood materials allow for exact color matching to related fixture finishes, and can be stained, painted, or stenciled to repeat design elements or even the bookstore's logo. Some of the new, super-strong finishing agents (polyurethane) and prefinished, acrylic-impregnated finishes are as durable as traditional finishing-in-place methods, making wood flooring as practical as it is beautiful.

Ceramic Tiles. Ceramic tiles have long contributed to the ambiance of bookstores. Unglazed ceramic tiles offer a warm and natural look, and many new products incorporate stains and dyes to produce colors never before available in an unglazed tile. Glazed ceramic tiles offer a wide variety of accent color and design possibilities, including solid colors, a granite look, or even a whimsical, active terrazzo look.

Marble and Granite. Generally more affordable than real marble, agglomerate marbles and granites are, in addition, often easier to maintain. Agglomerate marble offers new design and color opportunities. Terrazzo-like agglomerates featuring multicolored accents of glass and metal can be used to create a unique statement in flooring. Granite can be polished, flame-treated, or ground into tiles as thin as three-eighths of an inch. Marble and granite of various thicknesses are used for counter tops and table tops, as well as for floors.

Vinyl Tile. New vinyl tile and vinyl composition tile (VCT) products in both individual and sheet form are available in bright solids, non-directional and terrazzo patterns, confetti colors, and stone and wood looks. With accent stripes and a little creativity and imagination, VCT can be used to produce an upscale, durable, and inexpensive floor finish.

Rubber Base. Rubber base is available in many colors and in 2-1/2" and 4" heights. Topset coved rubber base can be used with VCT; straight-edge rubber base is made for use with carpet.

Concrete. Exposed concrete is used as a new, minimalistic design element to create discount-warehouse looks. Staining, sandblasting, and inlaying materials, such as

Ceramic tile and wood flooring meet at book walls, arches and alcoves made with custom store fixtures. Charlesbank Bookshops & Cafe', Boston, Mass.

metal, stone, glass, and straw, can create strong images. Exposed concrete floors do require some upkeep (a surface-applied sealer) to keep them looking great.

Programming Ceiling Design Elements

A beautifully designed and coordinated ceiling adds significantly to the interior ambiance of a bookstore. More ceiling area is exposed to customers than any other surface in a retail bookselling setting.

Commercial ceiling surfaces programmed for retail bookstore use are either attached to the structure or hung (suspended) from supporting systems. The ceiling conceals HVAC (heating, ventilating, and air conditioning), electrical, sprinkler, telephone, computer, security, sound system, and other utility lines. Each must be properly located, installed, and tested before the finished ceiling is installed.

Aesthetic Considerations. The surface, texture of material, and design of a ceiling must be appropriate to the theme of the interior. If beams, graphic elements, store fixtures, valances, video monitors, or kids' design motifs are to be secured to the ceiling, structural supports must be installed.

Space permitting, the ceiling may be raised or lowered, and coved elements added over aisles, selling or service areas, departments, or shops. Lighted cove ceilings can be a source of indirect light and are used to draw attention to selected spaces. High ceilings create a sense of value, low ceilings a sense of intensity.

Exposed Ceilings. The option to expose the ceiling structure and to paint out exposed surfaces and utility lines visible to customers can create an interesting image. Exposing wood rafters in a barn, attic, factory, or loft conveys an image of openness. An exposed steel or concrete structure ceiling can create a minimalistic effect. Leaving the ceiling and a cobweb of pipes exposed in a basement and painting the pipes an eerie lunar green for use over a children's department can help to create a fun and mysterious atmosphere.

Programming Ceiling Surface Materials

A variety of materials are available to finish bookstore ceiling surfaces. The most common are lay-in acoustical tile, gypsum board, wood, metal, and plaster. All are set in or attached to suspended ceiling systems. Each of these surfaces can be treated in a variety of ways: with applied mouldings, beams, coves, paints, or custom ceiling tile products.

Lay-In Acoustical Ceiling Tile. Ceiling tiles can be installed in suspended, 2-by-2-foot or 2-by-4-foot metal grid systems, leaving the metal grid exposed, recessed, or concealed. Panels of ceiling tiles can be designed to meet special acoustical and fire-resistant ratings. These panels are available faced with polished metal, vinyl, or fabric material, mirrored, or made of moulded plastic facings. Lay-in ceiling systems allow flexibility in the rearrangement of lights and mechanical utilities. They also provide easy access to the space above the ceiling.

Fixed Ceiling Tile. Ceiling tiles can be glued to smooth ceilings or stapled to wood furring strips that are attached to ceiling systems. These tiles, generally 12 inches square, have smooth or tongue-and-groove edges that can produce either a geometric grid or a continuous surface when installed.

Gypsum Board. Gypsum board, also called sheetrock, is durable, rigid, available in different thicknesses, and can be highly fire resistant when layered. Its surface can be smooth or have texture, which can be light or heavy and can be applied by hand or sprayed on. Gypsum board can be painted or not. If the finish is smooth, it can have wood moulding, vinyls, papers, and other finishing materials applied to it.

Wood. Wood decking, installed as a floor-over-ceiling on floor joists, can be left exposed to create a wood ceiling for the space below. Tongue-and-groove assem-

White tile floor, white sales fixtures and walls, and white three-dimensional Romany-pattern ceiling tiles in a sideline department. UNL Nightingale Bookshop, Lincoln, Neb.

ABOVE: Wood beams with raised coffers set the tone of this neoclassic Georgian interior. The superior materials - fine wood floors, trim, cabinets, and brass chandeliers - reflect the quality of the book collection in this superstore. ABOVE R: Entrance to the general book department is through a reproduction of an English Georgian shop front based on a design by Thomas King, London, 1834. BELOW R: Customers riding up escalators may look into sections of the 180,000 title base of the main general book department. BELOW L: Dark wood, custom stained-glass window, leather chairs, and plants were specified for this scholarly book department. Charlesbank Bookshops & Cafe', Boston, Mass.

blies of various widths, stained or painted to the desired finish, are commonly used for such installations. Wood beams can easily be integrated into standard ceiling systems.

Beaded wood planks can also be applied to the ceiling to create a special Victorian Porch effect. Hung ceilings can be made with wood grids or grilles. Wood panels with applied moulding can be used to create Gothic and other historical theme ceiling effects.

Ornamental Metal Ceilings. Metal or tin ceilings were mass produced in the 1800s to imitate ornamental plaster without the cracking or damage to which the latter is susceptible, and to provide fire protection. These ceilings are reproduced today in a variety of patterns. Metal ceilings finished with paint, bronze, brass, aluminum, and plastic coatings can be used to effectively capture the spirit of historic and nostalgic environments.

Painted Ceilings. Except for fabric surfaces, all the ceiling surfaces described above can be painted. Painting is often an economical solution for older ceilings that have faded, become stained or discolored, and yet are in good condition. The types of ceilings most commonly painted are gypsum board, moulded plastic, and metal.

Plaster Ceilings. Plaster is one of the oldest forms of ceiling finishes. Durable, rigid, moisture-resistant, and fire-resistant, the surface of plaster can be smooth or textured and can be molded into many shapes.

Plaster is either attached directly to a structural wood, metal, or concrete frame of a ceiling or installed on a suspended system. Both applications require a sound subsurface, generally a metal lath system, to which the plaster is applied in several coats. Plaster can be painted, or, if it is smooth, can have vinyls and papers applied over it.

Skylights and Clerestories. Skylights and clerestories introduce natural light into the store and create interest and visual excitement. Skylights and clerestories must be glazed with heat-treated or laminated glass and are available in a variety of stained glass, mirror, and open metal-grid materials.

Programming HVAC (Heating, Ventilating, and Air Conditioning) Systems

Programming indoor air temperature and quality is essential for customer comfort. Both must be right for the customer to linger and browse. Bookstores that are too hot or too cold are simply not comfortable. For a bookseller concerned with customer comfort, an HVAC system can be one of his best friends. A comprehensive description of retail HVAC systems is found in Appendix I.

The entire, initial installed cost of an HVAC comfort system will range between $5 and $10 per square foot; operating costs of the system will be approximately 75 cents per square foot. The difference between the best and worst systems can be as little as $1 to $2 per square foot.

It is always best to program newer types of air diffusers because they look better, work better, and can be cleaned. Electronic controls with automatic night set-back features help to reduce energy costs. Larger, more sophisticated mechanical facilities may require energy management systems to provide for remote-control monitoring of comfort systems to keep customers happy and operating costs low. Many of these systems have a certain amount of self-diagnostic remote-control ability so that servicing can be accomplished quickly.

Programming Exits, Stairs, Elevators, and Escalators

Local and national fire codes for commercial buildings specify that there must be at least two separate exits per floor for use in an emergency. If one becomes blocked, the other can be used as an alternate escape.

Escalators, power-driven stairs, are a merchandising asset capable of safely moving thousands of people up and down five of seven floors. Charlesbank Bookshops & Cafe', Boston, Mass.

Exits are primarily designed for use in an emergency. The location of exits is determined by occupancy load and fire resistance of the structure. Codes for corridors and doors along exitways govern their minimum width, maximum length, direction of door swing, and other features. Codes also specify details about tread and riser sizes, handrails, landings, construction, and related features of exit stairways.

Elevators and Lifts. Multi-level bookstores require elevators and lifts programmed for the movement of stock, customer traffic, and disabled and handicapped people, both the public and staff members.

Elevators can be designated as passenger or freight, or as a combination of the two. Elevators are either fully enclosed or have glass walls for view and style. Programming must address the elevator-cab finishes, call buttons, and lighting. Space must be programmed to accommodate the elevator, its electrical motors and hydraulic pump, and the machinery needed to operate the lift.

Dumbwaiters. A dumbwaiter, another form of elevator, is a small cab used only for moving freight. The largest allowable dumbwaiters, known as wheeler lifts, can be programmed with doors that open at floor level to easily accommodate book carts. Dumbwaiters can be electrically powered or manually driven.

Escalators. Escalators are electrically powered moving staircases that carry an endless stream of passengers. They can become a strong design element in a bookstore space. Escalators are generally installed in pairs, one up and one down to each level, although some stores provide escalators up and stairs down for economy. Neither elevators nor escalators can be programmed as exit devices; each must shut down in the presence of fire or smoke.

Programming Mechanical Conveying Systems. Multi-level bookstores generally contain mechanical conveying systems to move books and other objects both vertically and horizontally. Depending on their functions, electrically powered and gravity conveyors are programmed to move books and stock considerable distances, for example, from delivery trucks to back-room processing tables that are often on another floor. Conveyors provide an inexpensive alternative to a second (freight) elevator.

Programming for Building Codes and Requirements

The construction of bookstore buildings and their interiors is governed by many building codes, including the Uniform Building Code, the Basic/National Building Code, the Standard Building Code, and the National Fire Protection Association (NFPA). Building in Canada is governed by the National Building Code of Canada. Most of these building codes follow general guidelines that are comparable in scope and intention. However, each local building department interprets the codes slightly differently and allows for variances.

Programming for Disabled and Physically Impaired Persons

The Americans With Disabilities Act (ADA) is in place at both the national and state levels. Regulations and requirements for barrier-free design can, however, vary from state to state, and between public/commercial facilities and private/residential facilities. Key points to include in the PDM Specs are access to and from parking, walkways, and ramps, as well as the building entry, corridors, doors, stairs, and special features, which will vary with the size and location of the store. Water fountains, signs, telephones, counters, checkouts, and emergency devices also must meet clearance, height, and material requirements for easy use by the physically impaired.

Many books and articles containing general guidelines to designing for barrier-free access have been published. For a copy of *The ADA Handbook*, the widely

Easy customer stairs, with a midpoint landing and a skylight. Olsson's Books & Records, Alexandria, Va.

adopted standard guide for creating barrier-free environments, contact: Equal Employment Opportunities Commission, 1801 L Street, N.W., Washington, DC 20057.

Programming Wall and Column Design Components

The character and image of each individual bookstore determines the amount and location of free wall-space in the entrance and in the selling area. Bookstores committed to a strong book image will probably program building walls, and sometimes columns, with floor-to-ceiling bookcases right up to the front entrance of the store. Wood paneling is used on wall spaces behind cashiers, on exposed end panels, and sometimes around columns. Slatwall, a flexible system of narrow, thin, acrylic shelves fit into snug grooves cut into plywood and particle board panels, can also be used to treat exposed wall and column surfaces.

Columns can be shelved and lighted, mirrored, plastered with a smooth or rough texture, enclosed with plywood and stained, or faced with drywall board and painted. Columns can also be covered with a textured vinyl fabric in a color and design pattern appropriate to the theme of the store.

Programming Freestanding Bookstore Building Designs

The PDM building program for renovation of a house or for building a new freestanding bookstore building are the same. Each program must address a number of variables: the function of the building, style of the structure, materials and structural systems, budget constraints, merchandising use, and building codes. The size of the building - the "footprint" the building makes on the site - is governed by zoning restrictions, floor area, number of floors, and configuration of the building.

Sidelines

The character of your retail enterprise will determine whether the back wall of the stationery and gift department or the wall space above greeting cards or magazine display fixtures will be merchandised or mirrored, paneled with wood or slatwall, treated with mouldings, graphics, paper, or vinyl fabric, or painted a harmonious color.

It is a good idea to keep the number of different textures and design themes used on wall surfaces to a minimum. The use of too many different design elements in the same area can be distracting and can overwhelm the books and merchandise that are displayed.

Programming Design Theme Changes

To program a special children's, map, gift, or other specialty section, find a natural breaking point to change the theme: a column, corner, or cornice. When there are no natural dividers, one can be created with a frame, baffle, or similar device. The important thing to be sure of is that each individual element contributes to the overall image of the sales area and that it builds and reinforces the character of the bookstore.

Programming Bookstore Design Themes

Unless you have a specific theme or idea in mind for the design of book departments and the store itself, it is best to let the books themselves be the predominant texture

Freestanding columns provided with slatwall inserts for merchandising-related reading, audio, video and computer cassetes, and similar products. Academy Bookstore, U.S. Military Academy, West Point, N.Y.

and theme of the design at this point in time. Special themes are developed during the design concept stage of planning, which we will discuss in Chapter 5.

Programming Historic Buildings for Adaptive Reuse

Adaptive reuse entails modification of an existing, historic building interior. Historic buildings are an important part of our nation's culture; they not only remind us of the past but also serve us in the present and will serve us in the future. Quality bookshops in historic buildings serve as focal points and can add to the visual quality of our communities.

Although the character of the original structure often remains, its new use can be entirely different from its original use. For example, the former west wing of Independence Hall was modified to serve as a new bookshop.

The PDM Spec for adapting a historic building space for bookstore use attempts to preserve the historical character of the building and the building's historical materials. If these two can be saved, the building can continue to serve as a historical legacy.

At KWA, adaptive reuse is the most enjoyable part of our professional practice. Our interior designers and architects who specialize in this type of work are sought nationally because of their expertise.

Programming Housekeeping and Operating Equipment Requirements

Both the equipment for operating the store and the space to house it should be addressed in the PDM Spec. Table 3.2 provides a checklist of housekeeping, operating equipment, and supplies, which will serve as a handy reminder of the basic items needed to open and operate your new bookstore.

The Mediterranean theme of Mizner Park shopping center called for an inviting tiled and covered colonnade around two sides of LIBERTIES Fine Books & Music. Boca Raton, Fla.

Table 3.2 Housekeeping and Operating Equipment Requirements Checklist

Sales/Office Areas:
Computer System
Cash Registers
Telephone, Music, and Security Systems
Office Furniture
  Secretarial Desks
  Arm Chairs
  Secretarial Chairs
  Stacking Chairs
  Waste Baskets
  Staplers
Smoking Urn (At Entrance)
Shipping Supplies, Shipping Scale
Microfiche Reader and Books-in-Print
Time Clock and Card Holders
Step-Stools and Seats
Fax and Copy Machines
Children's Furniture
Occasional Furniture
  (Round Tables, Chairs, etc.)
Tables, Chairs, Stacking Chairs (Store
  in back room for author events)

Back Room:
Trash Cans (20 Gallon)
Round-Top Waste Container
  (In Rest Rooms)
Slim Jim Counter Waste Baskets
Vacuum Cleaner and Extension Cord
Mop Bucket and Wringer on Wheels
Mop Rack and Mops
Janitor Broom and Dust Pan
Six-Foot Ladder
Book Carts
Bulletin Board
Cleaning and Rest Room Supplies

Staff Lounge:
Table, 36" Diameter
Stacking Chairs
Coat Rack
Counter for Refrigerator, Coffee-
  maker, and Microwave Oven

Programming Project Schedules and Timelines

The PDM Spec described to this point describes what we want to do and where the action will take place. The project schedule and time line establishes dates on which these events will be initiated and concluded. It also establishes who will be responsible for initiating and following each major activity through to completion. The sample schedule presented in Table 3.3 will give you an idea of a simple but effective format that has worked well for us hundreds of times.

Table 3.3   Operational and Facility Planning Timeline

Time in Weeks	Activities	Bookseller	KWA
1	Select Name of Store	X	
	Engage Store Planning Consultant	X	X
2	Form Legal Entity; Open Bank Account	X	X
3	Select Site; Bind Lease	X	X
	Develop PDM Spec		X
4	Reserve Telephone, Fax, and Modem Numbers	X	
	Engage Bookkeeping Service; Request Tax ID Number; Develop Chart of Accounts	X	
5	Join ABA; Attend ABA Booksellers' School	X	
	Prepare Block Plans		X
6	Contact Wholesalers and Publishers; Open Accounts	X	
	Select and Order Electronic Inventory Control and Management System	X	X
	Develop and Finalize Category, Book, Magazine and Newspaper Lists	X	X
	Prepare Schematic Plans and Design Themes		X
	Design Storefront Graphics and Signage		X
10	Make Working Drawings and Fixture Details		X
12	Request Bids	X	X
	Building Permits	X	X
14	Start Construction	X	X
	Order Book Inventory; Establish Store Opening Promotion and Advertising Plan	X	X
	Schedule Photography and Publicity Advertising	X	X
19	Fixture Installations; CRT, Computer, Telephone, and Music Installations	X	X
	Engage Staff; Train; Install Security	X	X
20	Receive, Process, and Shelve Stock	X	
21	Dry Run, Soft Opening	X	X
22	Grand Opening	X	X

Flooring, walls, ceiling, lighting, stained glass, and fixturing details of this English, Georgian shop were established in the initial PDM specifications. Charlesbank Bookshops & Cafe', Boston, Mass.

Conclusion

Le Corbusier, one of the world's greatest architects, is credited with saying, "The better the program, the better the result." In our experience, the better everyone involved understands the final goal, the better the chance for success, for completing on time, and for meeting the marketing and merchandising needs of the new store.

We are finally there, ready to translate our new store from a word picture to graphic plans, one of the most interesting parts of the planning process - the part where imagination and merchandising creativity really take place.

Now, let's put the pencil to paper and plan the new store.

CHAPTER 4
BOOKSTORE PLANNING

The business of a bookstore is to sell books and sidelines. The purpose of bookstore planning is to develop a concept to sell as many books as possible in the shortest amount of time in a given location.

A flow-chart of a bookshop would simply be a functional cube with two open ends. At one end is book/merchandise inflow; at the other end is the inflow of customers. If the store is well planned, books and customers will meet in the middle. The inflow and control of books is a complex process, but it holds no mysteries that cannot be solved by a well versed organization. Attracting a continuous inflow of customers is a fine art; it calls for providing the best possible planning arrangements, as well as a smattering of showmanship and psychology. Although the scale and business emphasis may vary, the fundamental objectives for the smallest bookshop and the largest store are the same.

Planning Objectives

The principal objectives of the bookstore plan are to (1) attract customers into the store with an inviting storefront, (2) create an attractive, efficient, profit-producing selling space, and (3) integrate sales space with functional facilities to provide offices, staff amenities, and a back room with ample space to process the movement of inventory in and out of the store.

Organization

Bookstores are located in spaces and buildings of almost every size and configuration imaginable. You may already have bought a building or leased a new store space. If not, we can help locate an existing interior space that appears to be appropriate (see Appendix II). KWA provides the initial feasibility studies to confirm the suitability of the location and to present its pros and cons. We can also provide input for the initial stages of designing new bookstore buildings. We team up with local architects, engineers, and other design professionals to plan a building that will have the functional interior requirements of a bookstore.

Planning Activity

The first activity of planning is to analyze the existing or proposed building's storefront, interior space, and plans. If drawings are not available, the space must

Space for browsing/sale tables, service desk, and high floor gondolas beneath an antique skylight was planned to create the ambiance of a law library in this professional bookstore. New York University Professional Bookstore, N.Y.C., N.Y.

be accurately measured and a plan of existing conditions drawn to scale. During this process, we check the entrance placement and confirm available floor-to-ceiling heights, freight entrances, exits, and code restrictions. We also check on the sprinklers and the electrical and mechanical services of the building to determine the viability of the site. These existing conditions drawings establish or confirm the size of the space and its usable square footage. The plans that result delineate the location of such features as building elevators, stairs, rest rooms, communication links, and utilities.

Planning Components

Parking, Walkways, and Ramps. A convenient location, an adequate number of parking spaces, and proximity of parking to the bookstore entrance are of prime importance. Designation for handicapped parking must be provided and clearly identified, and the area must be policed. Pathways leading from the parking lot or street to the store entrance must have a hard surface, be free of obstructions, wide enough to accommodate a wheelchair, and otherwise made safe for the user. Ramps with handrails and minimum grade change are mandatory. Low-sloped ramps are a further benefit to the elderly and those using crutches or other assisting devices. Adequate night lighting is also important.

The Entrance and Entry. It is important for customers to get a good general impression of as much of the interior as possible while still in the entrance area or as they step off the stairs, elevator, or escalator on an upper floor. The entrance may be a simple opening in an enclosed mall, or consist of double doors and a vestibule in a strip center or freestanding building. The entrance area has several functions: it can give a sense of spaciousness to a bookstore, provide a meeting place for customers, and act as the introduction to a bookstore's customer amenities. The choice of whether or not to provide an entrance vestibule is a matter of practicality. In cold regions, it is almost a necessity. Overall, the design of the entrance should be reassuring to customers. Once customers are inside the bookshop, it is the function of the indoor sales area to make them comfortable and present them with as much ambiance, information, and impulse merchandise as possible.

When it is expected that shipments will be received through the front door, entrances should be located so that incoming stock-delivery traffic will not interfere with the flow of outbound customer traffic.

Aisles and Circulation. The layout of aisle and circulation space provided for customers and staff depends on the bookstore's style. The size and shape of the store will determine whether there will be a single main aisle or several main aisles. In a small bookstore, a straight, focal-end aisle may be all that is possible. In stores with larger floor areas and more complex merchandising programs, a centralized main aisle with branch aisles to disperse shoppers through the sales area is an effective layout. If the store is very large, and multi-level, the main aisle must provide easy access to the stairs, escalators, or elevators. Access to the back room, staging areas, and fire exits must always be clear and well defined.

Customer comfort, stock movement, and display visibility must be carefully considered when determining the width of aisles. Main aisles five to seven feet wide allow some degree of aisle merchandising. Twelve to fourteen feet permits aggressive merchandising and ample customer space. When space exists, it is a good idea to place sale tables, towers, or whales in the middle of the main aisle. Some state building codes and ADA specifications require the space between the aisle selling fixtures and wall units to be at least three feet wide (four feet is the preferred minimum) particularly where rolling ladders are used. Cross aisles four to five feet wide are best, although in reality, aisles are frequently narrower by about 10 to 15 percent.

It is desirable for a bookstore to be crowded sometimes, but a customer who

Compact mini-office, and service desk/cashier station with provision for self service and controlled sales. Boston University Medical Bookstore, Boston, Mass.

is jostled and feels closed in or lost will usually want to get out of the store as quickly as possible, and more important, not come back!

Customer Traffic Circulation and Adjacency Analysis

Customer Traffic Circulation. Bookstores must be designed for constantly circulating customer and service traffic. Customers are always on the move, walking and looking, up to the actual point of sale at the cash registers. To make this an easy and pleasant experience, we like to give customers a clear route between the store entrance and the interior sections of the sales floor, and from there back to the entrance. We plan these aisles so that customers can easily do what they enjoy, enter, browse, select, buy, and leave. The best circulation patterns in bookstores are arranged so that as customers move through the store, attractive visuals can be seen from any point along the aisle.

Adjacency Analysis. We begin by using the PDM specifications and feasibility study as a guide to relate the new store program to the floor plan. Graphic drawings are made to represent the physical relationships of the store needs. Adjacencies and functional relationships are then diagrammed and eventually transposed onto the block plan drawings, which address aisle-circulation network concerns and locate features and book sections in the best relationships. Block-planning adjacency and circulation patterns involve the movement of customers, inventory, and information.

Creative Adjacencies. The cross-merchandising of departments can increase sales. Combinations such as athletic equipment placed in the sports book department, or live plants or packaged seeds in the gardening book department are examples of creative cross-merchandising.

Access for the Elderly and Handicapped

Federal ADA and most state regulations require, with few exceptions, that access be provided for both the public and staff to all areas of retail stores. We think that this is also a matter of consideration for our fellow humans. Inclined ramps with a ratio of a 1-inch rise to 12-inch lengths, and steps with safety handrails must meet federal guidelines. Stairs, gentle inclines, and ramps are important for customer and functional access to raised platforms, changes in elevation at store entrances, and other special situations.

Vertical Circulation and Movement

Vertical circulation is critical for stores with sales, service, and office areas located on several levels. Well designed and inviting stairs can overcome the customer's objections to walking up or down. Customer stairs that lead to other selling levels require special design attention. One technique that holds interest on stairs is the mirroring of the wall side of the opening so that the sales displays on the other floors of the store are visible all the way up or down. Another technique is to line the stair well with photos of authors, new-book release posters, and book shelves, a treatment favored by British booksellers.

Stairways and Escalators. Stairways and escalators are best located either at the back or about two-thirds of the way back on the right side of the first-floor selling area. Customers walking to or from stairs and escalators thus situated are exposed to most of the main floor offerings before walking up or down to another level. Fire exits, as well as open customer stairways and escalators, must lead directly from the interior to the exterior. The size, location, and number of enclosed fire stairs and exits are stipulated by local ordinance.

Customer stairs are the principal means of vertical access to this store's four floors. Tattered Cover Book Store, Denver, Colo.

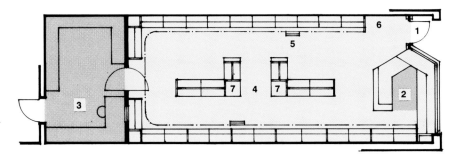

Brian Prince Booksellers - Scheme "C," Hamilton, Ontario, Canada. *(1) Entrance; (2)cash wrap, special orders, service desk; (3) back room, office with step display; (4) general and reference books; (5) rolling ladder and rail system; (6) feature wall display; (7) sales tables.*

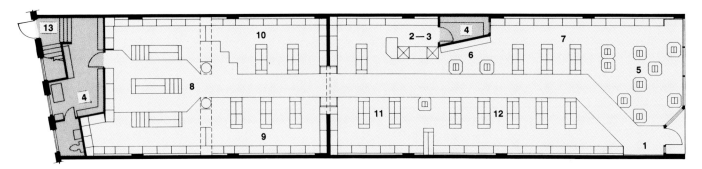

Charlesbank Bookstore, Wellesley, Mass.
(1) Entrance; (2) cashiers; (3) service desk; (4) back room; (5) NYT hardcover bestsellers; (6) cards; (7) audio, fiction & literature, mystery, science fiction; (8) children's; (9) health, psychology; (10) sports, travel, hobbies, games; (11) art, home, cooking; (12) business, computers; (13) stairs down to reserve.

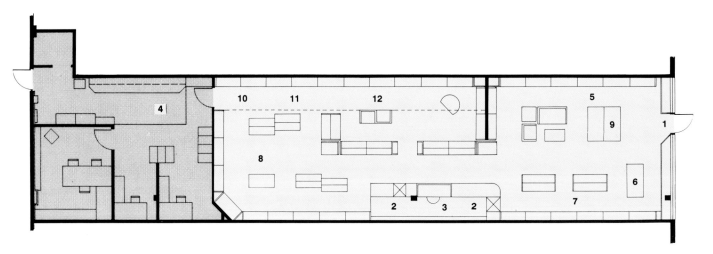

Barclay Booksellers, Allentown, Pa.
(1) Entrance; (2) cashiers; (3) service desk; (4) offices/back room; (5) NYT hardcover bestsellers; (6) bargain books (7) audio, fiction & literature, mystery, science fiction; (8) childrens; (9) new releases; (10) sports, travel, hobbies, games; (11) art, home, cooking; (12) business, computers (13) browsing, author signing area.

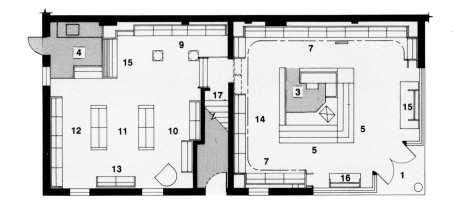

C. Johnson Bookseller, Ontario, Canada.*(1) Entrance; (2) cashier; (3) service desk, office; (4) back room; (5) hardcover bestsellers; (6) art; (7) fiction & literature, mystery, science fiction; (9) health, psychology; (10) sports, travel, hobbies, games; (11) gardening, home, cooking; (12) business; (13) science & nature, reference; (14) history, biography, religion, social science; (15) new releases; (16) magazines; (17) stairs down to basement, reserve.*

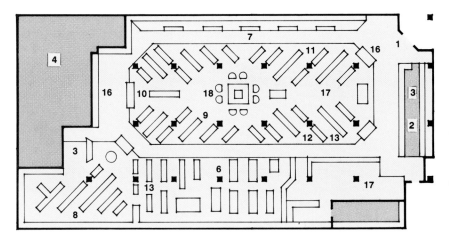

EARTHLING BOOKSHOP, Santa Barbara, Calif. *(1) Entrance; (2) cashiers; (3) service desk; (4) offices/back room; (5) NYT hardcover bestsellers; (6) bargain books; (7) audio, fiction & literature, mystery, science fiction; (8) children's; (9) health, psychology; (10) sports, travel, hobbies, games; (11) art, home, cooking; (12) business, computers; (13) science & nature, reference; (14) history, biography, religion, social science; (15) new releases; (16) magazines; (17) cafe; (18) fireplace.*

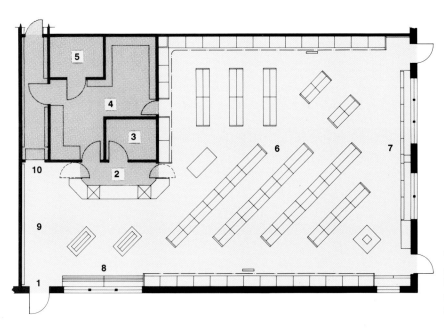

Wit & Wisdom Bookstore, Lawrenceville, N.J. *(1) entrance; (2) cashiers/service desk; (3) office; (4) back room; (5) rest room; (6) general & reference books; (7) children's books; (8) greeting cards; (9) magazines; (10) coffee bar.*

Raised Galleries and Podiums. Sales space can be made more effective by raising selected areas up to an appropriate height and onto a gallery. The height of gallery levels varies from eight inches to four feet. Consecutive galleries, raised one above the other, can also be employed to achieve greater efficiency in the use of space. Raised galleries add considerably to the interest of plan arrangements.

Cash Wrap, Information and Service Desks

Cash wrap stations and most service desks generate considerable traffic. Deciding on the best location for the cash wrap is always a serious matter. Cashiers' stations should be placed on the left side of the entrance. Why? Traffic flows to the right on the way in and on the way out.

The policy of the bookstore will determine the functions and services of the cashiers. When their basic function is to provide information, ring up transactions, wrap purchases, and make charges, small, L-shaped checkout units or straight counters are usually satisfactory. Bookmarks, audio cassettes, and other impulse sale items can be conveniently merchandised from cashier stations. When a bookstore retails these specialties, they are often displayed on or near the cash wrap.

Other customer service functions, such as receiving payment on charge accounts, making charges, taking and holding special orders, accepting telephone orders, processing lay-away orders, and gift wrapping, require larger cashier stations. Very large stores may relegate these activities to service desks located elsewhere in the establishment.

Special Order, Customer Service, and Information Desks

Special order, customer service, and information desks can also act as a magnet to draw customer traffic to interior locations in the bookstore. In large stores, we purposely locate these customer services in the rear, away from the cash wrap, to one side or even on upper or lower floors. Service desks require provisions for CRTs, ROM-CDs, microfiche readers, reference books, storage space for books and merchandise awaiting customer pickup, store telephone and paging instruments, sound and video system controls, and an appropriate number of service bookshelves and files. It is also where large children's stores keep the helium bottles used to blow up balloons.

Impulse Sales. Although more and more attention in general retailing is being given to capturing impulse sales, the average bookstore has barely scratched the surface of this opportunity to increase volume. Scientific store planning and merchandising can help take full advantage of every square foot of sales space to capitalize on impulse buying. The economic success of a store often depends on how well it stimulates these impulse sales. If a store sells only demand or convenience merchandise, which its customers plan to buy before they enter the store, it could soon be in bankruptcy. Buying surveys by one major book-selling group have shown that over 50 percent of all book sales it rang up were impulse sales. This means that their customers made more than half of their purchases without having planned to do so. Every store's newspaper advertising of staple merchandise and bargain sales should be calculated to bring in customers seeking both demand and convenience merchandise. Impulse sales can be the real benefit gained in the process.

Planning the Interior Selling Space

Apportionment of Space. The size and location of independent-bookstore selling and non-selling activities is based on sales forecasts and selling techniques.

The departmental sales forecast is the estimated number of units of merchandise (books) each department must have on the floor at one time to reach the sales forecast. The type of selling techniques the store plans to use can include personal,

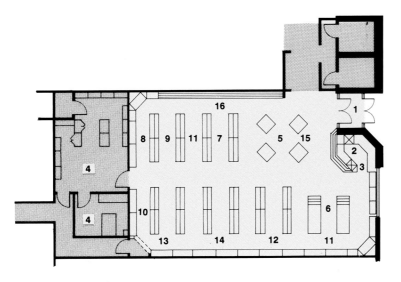

Pacific Stars & Stripes Bookstore, Osan A.F.B., Korea. *(1) Entrance; (2) cashiers; (3) service desk; (4) offices/back room; (5) NYT hardcover bestsellers; (6) bargain books; (7) audio, fiction & literature, mystery, science fiction; (8) children's; (9) health, psychology; (10) sports, travel, hobbies, games; (11) art, home, cooking; (12) business, computers; (13) science & nature, reference; (14) history, biography, religion, social science; (15) new releases; (16) magazines.*

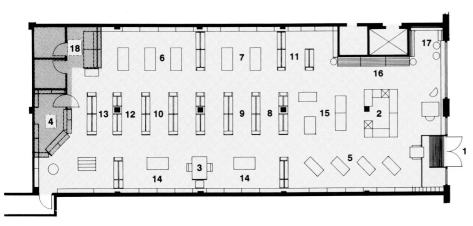

Discount Book Mart, Boston, Mass. *(1) Entrance; (2) cashiers; (3) service desk; (4) back room; (5) NYT hardcover bestsellers; (6) bargain books; (7) audio, fiction & literature, mystery, science fiction; (8) children's; (9) health, psychology; (10) sports, travel, hobbies, games; (11) art, home, cooking; (12) business, computers; (13) science & nature, reference; (14) history, biography, religion, social science; (15) new releases; (16) magazines; (17) cards; (18) open work station.*

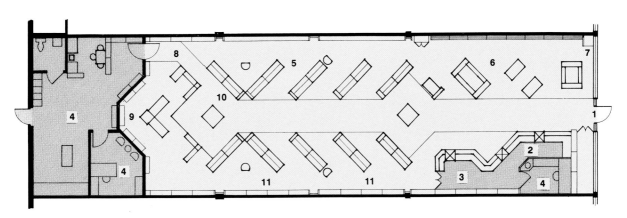

Moody Bookstore, Chicago, Ill. *(1) Entrance; (2) cashiers; (3) service desk; (4) offices and back room; (5) Christian adult fiction; (6) Moody Bestsellers; (7) gifts and cards; (8) Sunday school curriculum; (9) children's; (10) feature sales; (11) Bibles.*

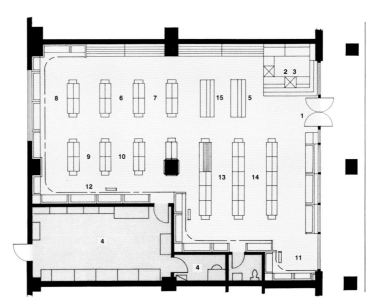

Pacific Stars & Stripes Bookstore, Yokosuka, Japan. *(1) Entrance; (2) cashiers; (3) service desk; (4) offices/back room; (5) NYT hardcover bestsellers; (6) bargain books; (7) fiction & literature, mystery, science fiction; (8) children's; (9) health, psychology; (10) sports, travel, hobbies, games; (11) art, home, cooking; (12) business, computers; (13) reference; (14) history, biography, religion, social science; (15) new releases; (16) magazines.*

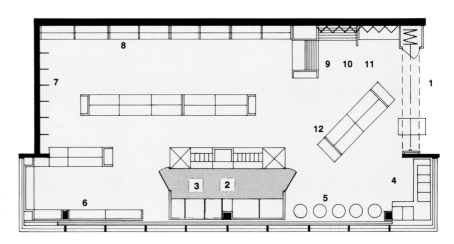

Leslie College Bookstore, Cambridge, Mass. *(1) Entrance - movable storefront; (2) cashiers; (3) service desk; (4) gifts; (5) cards; (6) general trade books; (7) seasonal apparel; (8) convertible textbook wall; (9) magazines; (10) paper-bound books & newspapers.*

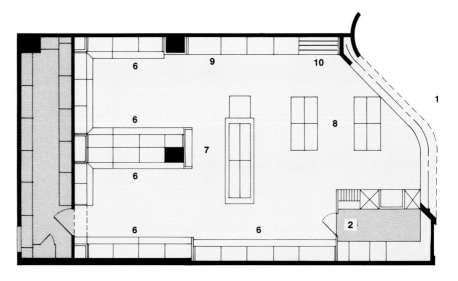

Boston University Medical Bookstore, Boston, Mass. *(1) Movable store front entrance; (2) raised cashiers & service desk; (3) back room; (4) NYT hardcover bestsellers; (5) bargain books; (6) medical reference; (7) medical textbooks; (8) school supplies; (9) gifts & apparel; (10) magazines; (11) fine pens, instruments.*

hand selling (expensive books, limited editions, pens), selling from samples (engraved stationery, imprinted Christmas cards), and self-selection (general books, supplies, art materials, novelties, imprinted t-shirts, gifts). These variations affect the choice of size of store fixtures, space for customer and service movement, amount of space to be allocated to feature displays, services offered, size of staff, hours of operation, and office requirements.

Book Categories and Sales Departments. Locating key book category merchandise in the front, center, rear, or sides of the store is based on (1) the need for the item to be visible in a primary location, (2) category adjacency, (3) customer convenience, (4) stock requirements, and (5) impulse sale value. High-impulse merchandise is best located in the vicinity of entrances, service desks, and cash wraps, the most heavily trafficked areas and the places where most customers congregate.

Adjacency of Categories. Book categories and sideline departments should be placed in logical relation to one another, arranged in a shopping pattern that makes it easy for the customer to find a book, and designed to generate suggestive selling. Art should be placed near Photography, History near Sociology, Cooking near Hobbies and Home Repair. Because of physical limitations, however, it is not always possible to establish ideal category relationships.

To draw traffic through the store, departments with greatest area demand and support requirements, such as children's books, are usually placed far from the entrance and on either lower or higher levels. The location of author signing and reading event areas and large reference departments also fall into this category. Magazines and newspapers, on the other hand, which tend to be impulse purchases, work best at the front right side of the store.

Non-Selling Facilities. Work stations, administrative offices, employee facilities, and related areas are always placed in secondary locations. Placement of non-selling areas will have a considerable effect on the shape and use of the surrounding selling departments.

The Back Room. The relationship of the back room to the sales area is important. It may be contiguous to the sales area in a small bookshop or located three levels away in a large store. The back room, which includes the receiving department and stock rooms, should relate to the sales area. The back room should be located close to the accounting office to facilitate the flow of paperwork. In some multi-store situations, books are received in a central receiving facility and then delivered to the bookstores. Adequate space is needed to open, unpack, count, check, verify the price of, and occasionally label incoming books and sidelines. Space for CRT terminals, filing shipping documents, and for processing return shipments is essential. A hold area is also required to store books, merchandise awaiting price or other processing information, and a reasonable quantity of store bags, supplies, and used shipping cartons kept on hand to facilitate returns.

Book Reserve Storage

When book reserve stock is required, it should, if possible, be located immediately adjacent to the selling area. Perimeter stock rooms are commonly found in college bookstores. The amount of book reserve space will vary with the size of the bookstore, amount of inventory to be processed, variety of merchandise, and frequency of deliveries.

Rest Rooms, Break Rooms, Lockers, and Staff Lounges. Small book shops generally have one rest room, a drinking fountain or stand with bottled water, and a coat rack or bank of employee lockers. There is usually a small refrigerator, a coffee maker, and a microwave. Larger stores may require more amenities. To find a break room with a full kitchenette, tables and chairs, drinking fountain, pay telephone, and coat lockers is not uncommon. Very large stores add candy, snacks, and hot and cold beverage vending machines. Separate men's and women's toilet rooms, equipped to meet handicap requirements, and an employee nap or rest room are required by many local health and building codes. Few book shops build or advertise public rest rooms unless they are mandated to do so by building ordinances. When public rest rooms must be provided, however, particularly in large, classic children's bookstores, we equip them with baby-changing stations.

How We Plan a Bookstore

We have illustrated how bookstore space is apportioned and discussed methods for locating categories and departments within the bookstore. The most practical way to help you understand the principles of the store planning process is to describe how KWA personally goes about the job of planning a bookstore, and, in passing, to indicate when our methods differ greatly from those of others whom we know.

Block Merchandise Planning

Using the PDM Specifications as the scenario, we begin by making a breakdown of the space into known requirements. This involves deciding how much area will be assigned to each selling and functional activity within the space available in the store. In the case of large stores, space is assigned to departments. During this important step in the planning process, we determine the amount of wall shelving or hanging capacity that the blocked-out area will accept. The remaining space in the department is then calculated to determine the number of appropriate store fixtures that it will contain. Provision is made at this stage for customer and service aisles. Most planners skip over this step and go directly from the block plan to the layout and arrangement of the store fixtures and service facilities. The weakness of that approach, however, is that the planners who follow this quick route may find themselves without adequate aisle capacity at the end of the plan and will have to start over again.

Next, we sketch and block out departmental areas onto several building plans drawn to 1/16-inch, 1/8-inch, or 1/4-inch to-the-foot scale. We use the plans to relate the adjacency of one merchandise department to the others. These plans are also useful to determine the best marketing, visual, and operational flow that we can devise for the store. Building plans are also used to relate associated non-selling and service areas with the sales area.

Our goal is to establish an efficient overall design based on a smooth, workable traffic layout. A floor plan that is forced to accommodate a particular motif can turn into an operational nightmare. Several different block plan layouts should always be prepared, all drawn to scale. They can then be used to review and discuss several possible planning solutions with you.

Overlays. In thinking out a plan for a bookstore, we try to imagine the people that will be using the store. We ask ourselves, "How will they perceive it?" Then we begin sketching the preliminary store fixture layout, working out the main areas, first with rough plans drawn at 1/16-inch to-the-foot scale on buff-colored sketching tissue, and then at 1/8-inch or 1/4-inch scale. These sketches are known as *overlays.*

As the preliminary overlays develop, the height of any selling area to be raised up onto a gallery and any changes in the height of ceilings are blocked in. As one cannot always visualize measurements exactly, we have a 2-inch-wide surveyor's rod (rule) running up the wall beside the door of our drafting room. This is divided into 1-foot sections in alternating colors with the footage nicely numbered. It is tremendously helpful to us in deciding such things as whether a cornice or an overstock fixture should be 7 feet high or 10 feet high. The rod helps us visualize the comparative height of the store fixtures that will border the raised galleries. When more merchandise is visible and accessible, main merchandising action

Clarion State University Book Center, Clarion, Pa.
*(1) Entrance; (2) cashiers; (3) service desk; (4) offices/back
room; (5) book check; (6) general & reference books; (7)
textbooks; (8) art & school supplies; (9) campus apparel;
(10) gifts; (11) Greek shop; (12) posters, cards; (13)
campus convenience store; (14) cold vault.*

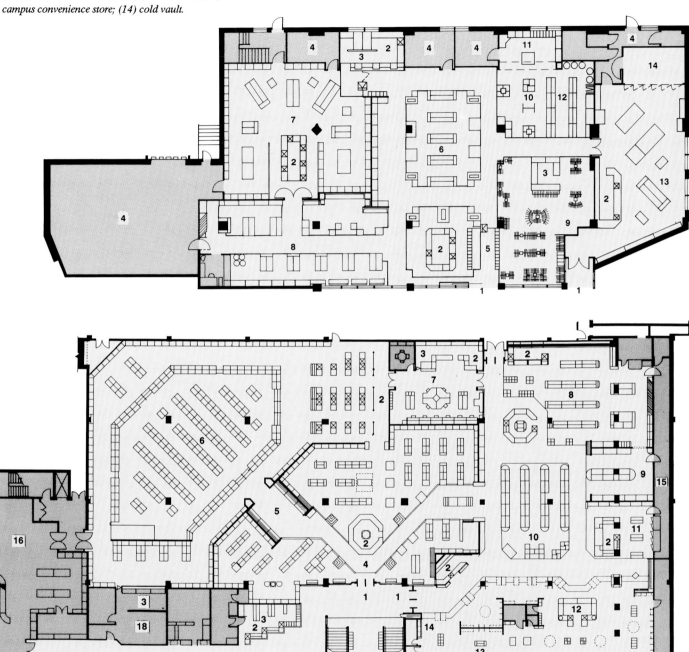

Nightingale Bookshop, Univ. of Nebraska, Lincoln, Neb.
*(1) Entrance - movable storefront & security system; (2)
cashiers; (3) service desks; (4) Nightingale Bookshop; (5)
magazines; (6) text books; (7) computer department; (8) art
and supply department; (9) dorm shop; (10) card, gifts;
(11) candy, snacks; (12) apparel department; (13) children's apparel; (14) insignia shop; (15) reserve stock; (16)
back room, processing; (18) offices; (19) buy back; (20)
copy shop.*

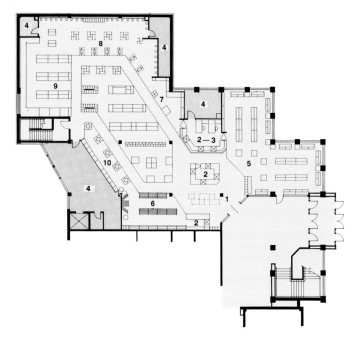

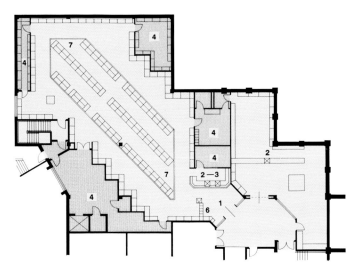

University Store, Millersville State Univ., Lancaster, Pa.
*Upstairs: (1) Entrance; (2) cashiers; (3) service desk; (4)
offices/back room; (5) general & reference books; (6) cards,
prints, posters; (7) computing; (8) campus apparel; (9) art
& school supplies; (10) gifts.*

*Downstairs: (1) Entrance; (2) cashiers; (3) service desk; (4)
offices/backroom; (5) book check; (6) new & used textbooks; (7) copy shop.*

usually takes place deep in the store at the point where major customer aisles intersect. These points become the locations for employing endcaps, steps, slatwall, or similar imaginative visual merchandising concepts. All the best ideas on the overlays are collected, neatly sketched, and lettered onto a single finished plan drawing.

Schematic Store Fixture Plan

When the departmental adjacencies and circulation paths have been established on the block plan and the ideas reviewed with you, the next step in the planning process is to plot and arrange the schematic store fixture plan. Here, store selling fixtures, equipment, and service requirements are drawn to scale in merchandising arrangements, within the shapes and boundaries of the selling departments as determined by the block plan. We take care to order, arrange, and draw the schematic preliminary store fixture plans so that the distances correctly accommodate the customer aisles, the required number of appropriate sales fixtures, and the quantity of shelving required to stock the amount of inventory planned.

Coordinating Fixture Plans with the Building Construction Plans

When the basic merchandising plan concept is set and the sales and service areas are established, our thought and effort turns to coordination of the store fixture plan with the ceiling arrangement, changes in ceiling height, beams, valances, curtain walls, lighting, HVAC outlets, and sprinklers. The final preliminary plan will arrange and merge ramps, galleries, store fixtures, and major traffic arteries into a single statement. Examples of these plans are illustrated in the plans for bookstores on the pages that follow.

Coordination with Building Systems

Care must be taken when coordinating the placement of store fixtures with the various mechanical and electrical systems of a building. Fixtures should be positioned so as not to block heating, ventilating, and cooling registers and radiators. Clear space must be maintained in front of all electrical panel boards and exits.

Coordination is also needed to ensure that fixtures supporting telephones, computer equipment, lighted directories, and displays are close to wall or floor receptacles. Of particular concern are fixtures that require special floor outlets when they are located in the middle of a floor. These outlets are often more expensive and complex to install than wall outlets. They may require removal, relocation, or capping if the fixtures are later rearranged.

Both natural and artificial lighting must be coordinated with fixture placement in relation to shopper selection and browsing. For reading and browsing, we must ensure that, where possible, fixture placement and orientation are designed to take advantage of natural daylight and are augmented with artificial light. Special fixtures and equipment, such as video and computer screens, must be oriented so that there is no glare or reflection from windows or bright light sources. If strategic placement is not possible, a screening device must be used to alleviate these problems.

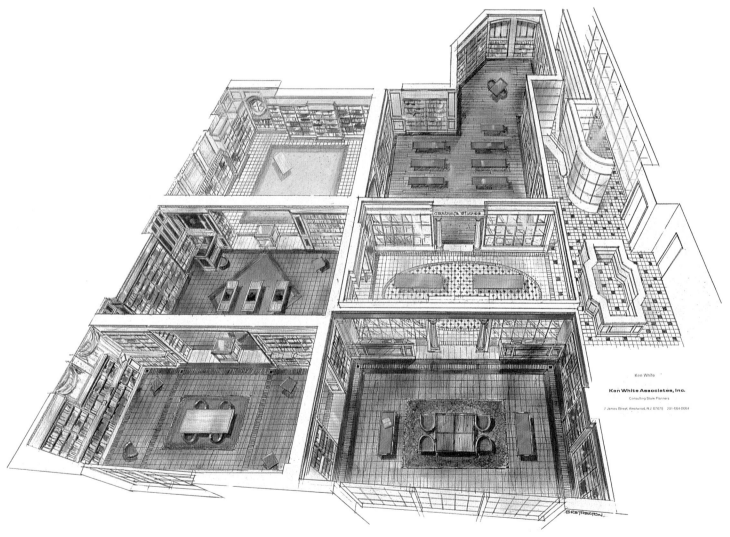

Bird's-eye perspective sketches are made to coordinate colors and finishes. They help everyone involved understand the scope of the project. Fifth floor, Charlesbank Bookshops & Cafe', Boston, Mass.

Design Sketches

As the plan is developed, we find it helpful to sketch out a number of bird's-eye views and normal perspective sketches of the principal aspects of the bookstore. These sketches are made so that we can visualize the way the elements of the plan and design will relate to the program as a whole and to one another. Many design sketches are simple line drawings, but others are a combination of ideas, and portray the contrasting qualities of each of the bookstore design elements. They preview the development of the character and ambiance of different sections of the bookstore.

Rendering Perspective Sketches. Design perspective sketches are part of the process and a means to an end. Our designers continually collect and sketch out informal ideas as they travel - at meetings, lunches, or on trains or airplanes going from one project to the next. These little sketches are drawn for the next step and later reference on whatever is at hand: napkins, business cards, flight-coupon jackets, or in notebooks or diaries.

Many of the perspective design drawings made by our staff of professional designers are truly works of art. Our designers work with a number of design and drawing styles. Their presentations range from a casual collection of delineated plans, line sketches, and color boards to finely detailed, richly colored, and shaded rendered elevations and perspective sketches.

Some bookstore projects require detailed perspective sketches with every shelf drawn in place in order to convey to the client the scope of activity that will occur in the scene illustrated. These sketches are often reproduced and used by booksellers to assign bays and shelves to book sections as the locations of basic book categories are planned.

Perspective sketches are drawn in a variety of art mediums. Black-line shadow and tone sketches are most commonly used because they are easily reproduced for advertisements, publicity, and a host of other purposes once the final design is established. Some designers prefer to draw with colored ink; others with pens, markers, or washes. Still others work with Conte crayons on colored paper or make full color illustrations with pastels, water colors, or tempera colors. Illustrations capture the spirit of design, are often imaginative, and always impressive.

Bookstore Plans

The preliminary designs described herein are developed to portray the merchandising, operational, and conceptual relationships of the project. The refined plan sketches, along with an updated budget estimate, are presented to you for input and approval before moving on to the next phase.

Design Development and Presentation Drawings

Following your approval of the preliminary design concepts, the store planning activity moves into the design development phase. Here, drawings and material selections become more specific as the character, size, and details of the entire project are determined. Appropriate finishes, store fixtures, and furnishings are studied and coordinated with the design concept. These elements are then assembled with careful draftsmanship, since we always present our best effort for each project.

The ideas and solutions we have developed in a presentation format are shown to and discussed with you in detail. Each project has a presentation style and format of its own. Some are very formal, with a theatrical flair, and others are more informal.

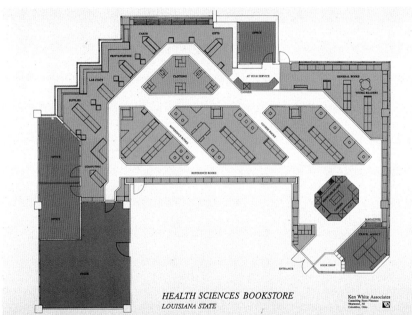

HEALTH SCIENCES BOOKSTORE
LOUISIANA STATE

Ken White Associates
Consulting Store Planners
Westwood, NJ
Columbus, Ohio

ABOVE: Rendering of proposed health-sciences bookstore for Louisiana State University in New Orleans. CENTER: Plan of proposed LSU health-sciences bookstore. BELOW: Rendering of medical book department in The Book Room, University of Toronto, Ontario, Canada.

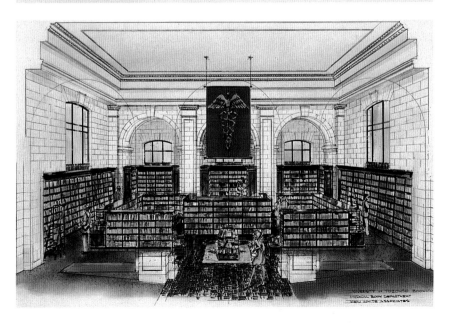

Updating the Preliminary Cost and Time Estimate Plan

When the preliminary store fixture plans and sketches have been made, the next important step is to review and update the estimate of costs and the time schedule of completing and opening the new bookstore. This is serious work, and often requires securing preliminary estimates of both cost and time from reliable fixture and specialty contractors. This procedure is a safeguard to both control cost and keep the project on target. If cost is excessive, this is the time to adjust the preliminary plans and scope of the work to bring the project back onto budget.

Modernization Planning

When existing fixtures are to be reused, they must be photographed, measured, surveyed, cataloged, and plotted onto a plan drawing. Thus, the newly prepared plan will provide an accurate view of the existing building and equipment. For remodeling projects, the conceptual planning process is the same as it is for a new bookstore. The detailed planning work involved in bookstore modernization is tedious, time-consuming, and often complex, but the results always make it worthwhile.

Techniques of Gaining Space

Extra stock capacity can usually be found for books and merchandise by extending wall cases to the ceiling, thus increasing shelf capacity. Book and merchandise gondolas can be double-decked, and wall shelving or glass cubes can be built around columns. The use of overhead book beams to extend stock shelving down from the ceiling to a height of 7 or 8 feet above the floor not only adds increased capacity but also contributes to the character and image of the bookstore interior.

Considerable space can also be gained by moving wall cases flush against the building wall between the projections caused by HVAC ducts, building pilasters, and pipes. Spaces between the recessed fixtures can be fitted with appropriate displays, adding to the selling power of the store. In other situations, column facings are covered with shelved wall cases to increase stock capacity or with mirrors to visually stretch the size of the space.

Planning and Designing with Store Fixtures

Designing bookstore interiors with fixtures is an integral part of the programming, store planning, and fixture selection processes; it is not simply a matter of arranging fixtures or choosing the types after the functional planning is complete. Although many of the details of exact placement and individual selection occur after the establishment of the space planning and design concepts, designing with fixtures occurs throughout a project. Fixture selection occurs at different levels of involvement throughout the design process, from the design of conceptual images and the determination of the functional needs of the pieces to their exact selection, procurement, and placement.

Bookstores organized to take advantage of good design, circulation, product adjacency, and impulse buying can provide comfortable, convenient shopping conditions for their customers. Easy traffic routes and attractive sales departments help to make shopping fun. When customers find that it is easy, convenient, and fun to shop in a bookstore, they will come back again and again.

Planning for Security

Theft of books is a serious problem. It has been believed for some time that the best form of theft protection is an alert staff, that is attentive to all customers

Theme tables and boutique-style visual merchandising presentation of Christmas books and calendars. The Book Nook, Wyckoff, N.J.

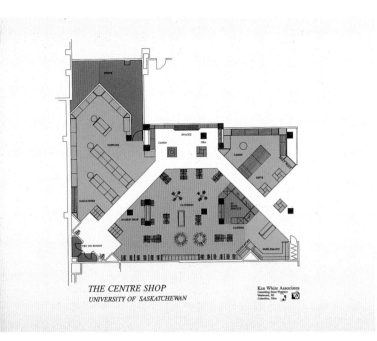

THE CENTRE SHOP
UNIVERSITY OF SASKATCHEWAN

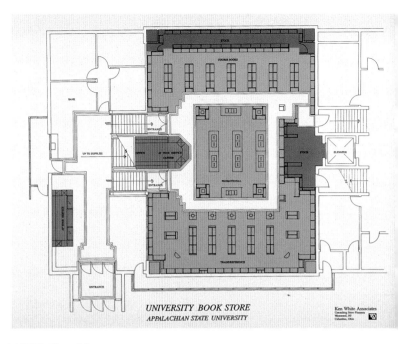

UNIVERSITY BOOK STORE
APPALACHIAN STATE UNIVERSITY

ABOVE: Plan of The Centre Shop, University of Saskatchewan, Canada. RIGHT: Plan of the scholarly book department, Appalachian State University, Boone, N.C.

entering the bookstore. This continues to be true for most small stores. But as the size of bookstores has expanded into large and multi-floor configurations, the cost of staffing large and often remote areas has soared. At the same time, shoplifting has increased over 50 percent during the last 5 years, according to the FBI's *Uniform Crime Report*, with one person in 15 entering a retail store to steal.

The store plan should be arranged to provide a comfortable traffic flow and spatial environment that does not impede store security. For small and large stores, we have the option to use raised checkout, office, and sales areas, or controlled fixture layouts and galleries with proper access.

Visual surveillance of the sales floor by staff members logically calls for low center-floor fixtures, approximately 4 feet 6 inches high. As stores generate more sales volume, however, there is a constant need to stock more titles. The result is that selling fixtures become taller, which in effect creates a series of cul-de-sacs, often with high aesthetic appeal but poor security, unless wide aisles can be provided between the stacks.

When a control or security problem is anticipated, mirrors, closed-circuit cameras wired to 72-hour VCR tapes, uniformed guards, and electronic surveillance systems can be employed. With these devices, shelf heights can be increased and more merchandise displayed for additional sales volume. Electronic surveillance systems are popular with libraries and an increasing number of independent, chain, and college bookstores. They are reported to reduce shoplifting by as much as 80 percent. Customers simply walk through a gateway in the proximity of the store's exit. If books and other merchandise have been properly charged, the customer exits smoothly from the sales area. But if the books or merchandise have not yet been paid for, a sensing unit is activated, sounding an audible alarm and alerting store personnel. Typical systems are activated by a strip of magnetic tape inserted in the spine of books, or by magnetized tags applied to general merchandise. This system is also used for screening personnel entering and leaving the store.

With the plan completed, let us now look at the factors that influence the design of the store.

CHAPTER 5

DESIGN CONCEPTS

Retail Bookstore Design

Some of the most exciting interior spaces in the retail world are found in today's general and independent bookstores. We include college and academic stores in this definition. The buying and selling of books, periodicals, and sidelines, as well as customer service aspects of retail bookselling, pervade our daily lives through aggressive advertising and specially built environments that invite us to spend our money. The marketing strategies and design of a bookstore are controlled by its location, the type of services or categories it sells, the price (discount vs. no discount), and the targeted customer profile. Retail outlets range from conservative to up-market to stimulating and playful children's and specialty bookstore environments. Academic bookstores are geared towards the retail of large quantities of books, the efficient handling of customer movement, one-stop shopping for a variety of goods, and the buying and selling of used books. Other stores are geared towards leisure shopping and a high level of customer service. Some specialty shops, such as arts and crafts, map, and travel stores, primarily market both books and related supply products.

Retail Ambiance

Through the effective combination of lighting, color, and physical environment, ambiance in retail design is created to enhance the display of books of every category and lead the shopper into buying. There are hundreds of styles of bookstores that are successful in their own unique settings. The style of decor and ambiance can range from quiet and elegant, to loud and brash, to quaint avant boga.

Bookstore Images

A successful retail bookstore design image is an array of design concepts that visually communicates to its customers that it is indeed a retail bookstore. The design image should convey the type and quality of the bookselling establishment, because what the exterior promises, the interior must deliver.

Interior and exterior image design elements and choices of materials should reflect the type and quality of books, merchandise, and services the bookstore will offer. The character of the exterior design and building materials should be consistent with the character of books and merchandise displayed and sold inside.

The image of a large, multistory university bookstore, for example, should convey to its various publics that it stocks a tremendous quantity of books and

We programmed philosophy books to rest side by side with belles lettres in the classics section of this superstore. Golden oak partner desks, wicker-backed armchairs, dictionary tables and black finished casework were used to create a library effect. Webster's Books, Ann Arbor, Mich.

ABOVE: Wood floors, panel ceiling, oak fixtures, oriental rug, and maroon leather upholstered browsing chairs where customers may relax and examine books. RIGHT: The Gothic-style entrance facade. FAR RIGHT: Oak columns share Byzantine-like incised, carved lettering shields and mouldings. The inner columns are sculpted with the heads of Jim Ward, then the university architect, Ken White, the store manager and others involved in the design of the shop. Gothic Bookshop, Duke University, Durham, N.C.

merchandise, and that it is part of the institution. Whether it is constructed of brick, stone, concrete, or metal, the materials and design elements of the bookstore should reflect the character of the campus.

The same holds true for a small, single-story, independent trade bookstore. The building may be rustic or contemporary, constructed of wood or a variety of other exterior materials, but it must reflect the style and tradition of its surroundings. This applies to all bookstores. At KWA, we approach bookstore design as the interpretation and synthesis of traditional and cultural elements with our clients' ideas for the desired ambiance.

Types of Bookstore Interior Design

Bookstore designs are logically divided into two basic concepts: theme and contextual.

Theme bookstores are created around a selected image or idea that appeals to our visual and intellectual senses of places, persons, things, events, or experiences. The design is created with the theme in mind; for example, a Gothic, Baroque, Georgian, or Victorian library may be chosen as the underlying, guiding principle from which everything else evolves. Unfortunately, theme interiors can be over-done to the point of triteness or can quickly become outdated. They can, however, be very successful and a delight to experience when they are subtle in design detail, leaving one's imagination to make strong thematic connections.

Contextual bookstore design concepts are based on contemporary principles and materials. They provide interior spaces and finishes that are supportive of the

ABOVE: Colonial Georgian motifs - small rectangular space, low ceiling painted white, cherry wood paneling and case work, leather chairs, brass lamp, oriental rug, and parquet floors - were used to create this area for author's signings. RIGHT: Neoclassic Georgian paneling and moulding details were painted white to blend with the ceiling. These columns and beam treatments add interest and help balance the design elements of the interior. UNL Nightingale Bookshop, Lincoln, Neb.

bookselling experience and do not create too artificial or theatrical an atmosphere. Contextual design has no distinct theme guides, just good, simple design that is conducive to the act of bookselling. The aim of contextual design is to evoke a customer response to the new store that says, "It feels fresh and wonderful. It's a great bookstore - we like it."

Aesthetic Design Characteristics

Bookstore design is a worldwide activity, an international language that encompasses many dialects. In the Far East, bookstore design is often imaginative, well done, and conditioned by the need to respond to cultural differences in customer buying patterns and service concepts. Bookstore design in England, Europe, Ireland, Mexico, and south Central America is more in line with the U.S., although each country has its own unique design elements. We can all learn from one another.

From the strident characteristics of mass-market retail outlets to the subtle specialized tones of more exclusive superstores, bookstore design speaks to people within all income brackets and with many different attitudes and aspirations. Graphics within most bookstore interiors are usually nothing more than sources of factual information. It is the major design components such as storefront fixtures, flooring, ceiling, lighting, and color that provide the ideas, opinions, and imaginings of language. It is their integrity and harmonious coordination that produce a meaningful ambiance and distinctive bookstore style.

Decoration for its own sake often leads to a disruption of design continuity and, in extreme cases, becomes pretentious. Our designers maintain a principle of expressing the structural and technical authenticity of both exterior and interior elements.

Bookstore Design and Image Agenda

When we begin to create the design of a bookstore, the first task is to establish an image vocabulary of shapes and colors and details and graphics. From that vocabulary we begin to create settings and images that say things. Sometimes we speak loudly, sometimes we speak softly, but what we must begin with is a visual code to complement the bookselling activity.

Many visual vocabularies are successful in bookselling. These include dozens of styles: casual, rustic, Western, colonial, traditional, Gothic, Georgian, Regency, classical, Victorian, art nouveau, and post modern.

The Basis of Bookstore Design

We do not share the belief of the modern movement in architecture that one has to break completely with history to be original. In the early 1980s, we started talking about the idea of bookstores that look like libraries in which books were for sale. The timeless appeal of the personal English, French, German, and Austrian library stems from its lived-in look. The library is by far the most lived-in room in the traditional English house. It is also the room that is constantly changing as its principle objects - books - are added or removed to be read and enjoyed.

For the first time since World War II, bookstore design themes that once were called "decorative" with the merest hint of a sneer have become highly important in bookstore design. And rightly so. Careful design based on classical themes is successfully being used to create market separation, and to attract up-market customers, who, psychologists tell us, yearn for the soothing settings of former eras.

Attitudes toward surroundings have changed. Classical and neoclassical design themes have been adapted by most superstore chains, which rely on demographic analysis. The conclusion that customers are attracted to the settings of the past is being borne out by both bookstores and parallel retail settings: museum shops, up-scale clothing stores, and restaurants - places that equate with the good life.

Whimsical themes built around storybook and comic book characters, and mood themes built around ideas can be successful, but they must be well done and well built to withstand the hard use that they will encounter.

Adapting Classical Themes to Current Conditions

The styles that most of us are familiar with are no longer a pure reflection of the historic style that inspired them. It is therefore not necessary to faithfully duplicate the woodworking details of an English library, an art noveau style Austrian shop, or a French Directoire salon (though that would be fun) to create an Old World aura in a new store. What is important is to impart enough traditional elements to create atmosphere. Period windows, entrance doors, and graphics, dark stained or lacquered woodwork, carpeting, old-fashioned incandescent light fixtures, and a rich, authentic color scheme can be combined to create a classical bookshop that is neither brittle nor delicate, but relaxing and unpretentious.

Quiet contextual architecture with well-executed traditional forms, textures, color, and lighting are preferred by most customers and booksellers. Booksellers generally prefer classical and period themes because of their longevity. Contemporary designs must be extremely well thought through and developed or they quickly assume, after five or so years, a tacky, cluttered look that is out of place, dated, and irrelevant. Balance and tasteful understatement are always a good solution that can be accomplished within a modest budget.

RIGHT: Daylight, plants and English step stools accessorize this comfortable book department. The design borrows dark wood and brass inlay, Edwardian details, to create the image of a quality bookseller at work. RIT Bookstore, Rochester, N.Y. *LEFT: Painted several values of gray, this neoclassic English Georgian entrance to the scholarly book department is symmetrical.* Charlesbank Bookshops & Cafe', Boston, Mass.

Classical Design Themes

The ability to achieve a sense of rightness in a bookstore, while still making it highly functional, is a real challenge. The final product must never be disquieting or off-putting. In this respect, successful, classically influenced designs differ markedly from many of the so-called postmodern stores of the last decade, where historical form was often contorted into something visually awkward. The illustrations in this book reinterpret classical forms to a degree that might once have been startling to think about, but are not startling at all to look at now.

There is no single source of reference for the design of classical storefronts or interiors. They must be interpreted from classical architecture of the style or period we are working with, whether it is Gothic, Georgian, Regency, Victorian, or art noveau. It takes taste, talent, and experience to capture the styles of the past and recast them into something that works today. We must be concerned as much with the intuitive visual rightness of a composition as with any kind of abstract theory. At the same time, bookstore design is just as dependent on stern realities such as the economy and the competitive climate as it is on atmosphere and the book selections offered to customers.

Contemporary Contextual Design Themes

Unless a store is designed and detailed exclusively in a particular style, all of the fixtures we select - regardless of their name tag - are contextually contemporary: they were made in today's world. The real issue is, how modern do you want your

store to be? The photographs within this book show many styles of bookstores from which you can discover the style of store you want to open and can live with.

Although we often interchange the terms *modern* and *contemporary*, the former is more accurately identified with the Bauhaus and international movements in design history. Designers and proponents of stark, contemporary bookstores (the architects of the Bauhaus), for all their importance to our culture, only occasionally produced work that can be said to be outstanding commercial successes. Bookstores and their buildings, by and large, are cerebral more than they are emotional. The majority of shoppers are simply not comfortable in stark contemporary or highly abstract environments.

ABOVE: View of the fireplace, where customers may relax in Windsor chairs with their books in a setting reminiscent of a ski lodge. The high raftered ceilings, a partially exposed brick wall and pattern carpet contribute to the warm feeling of this contemporary contextural design. Earthling Bookstore, San Luis Obisbo, Calif. *LEFT: Show window puts entire general book department on display. Rich wood floors, fixtures and front are combined with shadowed gold leaf lettering. The quiet background color was used to allow attention to be focused on the book presentation. This contemporary, two-floor college store is located in a historic building that was once a winery.* DeAnza Community College, Cupertina, Calif.

Computer-Aided Drafting and Design (CADD) techniques are employed in the planning and conceptual design of independent bookstores. Frank White, President, Ken White Associates, Columbus, Ohio.

Design Accessories

Classical design accessories have endured over the ages, whereas designs from other eras have been merely fads and have fallen from popularity. The enduring designs are considered classic and are still produced today. Fortunately, some manufacturers make inexpensive imitations that measure up to the originals in material, craftsmanship, proportion, and durability. There are many kinds of antiques which enhance the atmosphere of a bookstore. Grandfather clocks, old school desks, signs, posters, tables, and chairs can be incorporated into almost any design scheme as a feature or focal point.

Design of Espresso Bars, Coffee Houses, and Restaurants in Bookstores

Dining in bookstores can be big business today, and food facility design is probably one of the most innovative arenas for creating complementary interior environments. Most food facilities found in bookstores are simple, because they either are not expected to be long-lasting environments or need periodic remodeling. On the

ABOVE: Original design sketch illustrates how Viennese art nouveau coffee house styling was reinterpreted in the design of this smart 50-seat cafe'. LEFT: Etched glass, screen panels, art and stained glass valance. The walls and ceiling are enriched with mouldings. Marble table tops and Viennese-style velvet-upholstered cane-back chairs set the look. White tile set in a dotted pattern contributes to the ambiance. RIGHT: Art nouveau theme expressed in the entrance foyer of the Cafe' Charles. Charlesbank Bookshops & Cafe', Boston, Mass.

ABOVE: A large Trompe L'Oeil mural of famous authors sets the theme for the cafe' and contributes to the ambiance of this store. Barnaby Conrad, Artist. Earthling Bookstore, Santa Barbara, Calif. RIGHT: The spacious left front of this shop is zoned into a visually connected table-service coffee house and bookselling area. The area is defined by a low rail topped with live plants. Cane-seat, bent-wood chairs, live plants on wood tables, and a raised stage complete the high-end look. A beige backdrop for the food, flowers, books and customers unifies the space and ties the interior to the exterior architecture. You may order a cookie, muffin, baguette, bagel, or a light entree. There's strawberry cheesecake, coffees, teas, chocolates and juices. Canterbury Booksellers Coffeehouse, Madison, Wis.

other hand, food facility design can be complex, since most eateries must be specifically designed for a targeted market. Interiors should provide an appropriate atmosphere for the serving and consumption of food and beverages. Even if stunning interiors are created, however, the food facility may be doomed to failure if the marketing, management, and service to the customer falter.

Beyond serving food and providing a friendly, neighborly, or clubby atmosphere in the bookstore, coffee houses also furnish an arena for the see- and-be-seen needs of social life. People who patronize bookstore food facilities generally fall into one of four target groups. First, there is the eat-and- run type, who usually want a quick cup of coffee, a cup of soup, a salad, or a pastry. This type customer may find service and time savings more important than the price and quality of the food. The second type customer is the connoisseur, who wants excellent food. Price, time, and speed of service are not quite as important to this customer as having a quality meal. Third are comparative shoppers, who expect a balance of good food, reasonable price, and good service. These people tend to dine out dressed informally and often have children with them. The fourth type customer is the socialite, for whom dining in a bookstore is primarily a coffee klatch experience. This type customer may want to eat only a snack or light refreshment, and is also interested in entertainment: reading, dance, jazz, or old films.

The design of the bookstore food facility should correspond to the needs of these four target groups. Most establishments cannot be neatly categorized as catering to only one of these types. Some cater to more than one group, sometimes by changing their service delivery: for example, setting up a buffet at times but providing full tableside service at others.

Food facilities are expensive to build, and can be difficult to staff and operate. But they can also be fun - and profitable.

CHAPTER 6

CHILDREN'S BOOKSTORES

There are few independent bookstore sales categories or departments that lend themselves more to pure theater than the children's book department. Children's books can be sold as successfully in a simple, homey cottage living room as in an upscale environment.

A good children's bookstore plan requires adequate space. A customer may want a board book, a picture book, a teacher's aid, a classic or a novel, a reference, science, or activity book. Perhaps they can buy elsewhere for less money. But they go to their favorite children's bookseller - you - because the product comes complete with the human experience; a sincere smile at least, a friendship, and a good time without a doubt. From this point on, and for the sake of clarity, we will refer to Children's Sections and Departments as Children's Bookstores.

The Size of Children's Bookstores

Children's bookstores range from tiny shops 250 square feet to gigantic presentations of 4,000 square feet or more. The stock of these departments ranges from small select inventories of 800 to 1,200 titles to as many as 24 to 27,000 titles.

Space is indeed needed for the presentation of the product, for wide aisles, and for storytelling, lectures, demonstrations, and entertainment. Cash wrap stations are becoming larger; VCRs, music systems, CD-ROMs and POS terminals must be housed. More about this in Chapter 10.

Planning Considerations

Where do you begin to plan a children's bookstore? We suggest you begin with a mission statement, as defined in Chapter 1. Then follow each of the steps through Chapter 11 described in this book. There are no short cuts or easy ways to plan and build a successful children's retail facility. Children's bookstores, more than any other specialty bookstores, look deceptively simple but are indeed complex.

For one thing, there is a variety of sizes of children's books, ranging from the tiny "little books" first designed by Beatrix Potter to the jumbo workbooks, calendars, and activity books of recent years.

We must also decide which age groups your store will appeal to. Baby through early-year books have one set of problems. If your stock will include parenting, pre-natal to baby, and young adult books, that's another set of problems. All require space and in many instances specialty types of fixturing to properly display and merchandise the books and sidelines.

A single Doric column, soft lavender, beige and brass colors combined with green-lighted book graphics, placed on a shelf with sculpted book ends, create a special welcome in this wonderful small, children's bookshop in the Columbia Mall. Junior Editions, Columbia, Md.

ABOVE: In addition to children's books, there are rubber stamps, stick-ons and other sidelines available at the Junior Editions main service desk. The ceiling is flush and painted white throughout. The primary light source is the new, low-voltage, flourescent down-light. The flooring is a neutral red oak parquet pattern. ABOVE R: U-shaped gondolas are versatile. They create places to explore. Wall fixtures divide the space into two sales rooms. Ends of alcoves are sheathed with a narrow-spaced showall, a key part of the display. Face-out display is maximized. BELOW R: The focal elements in the design are closed-top castles that hold various groupings of children's books, a throne and intriguing sidelines. Junior Editions, Columbia, Md.

ABOVE: The storefront opens wide and tables and castered displays roll out into the mall. Field trips to the bookstore are scheduled events that kids really enjoy ... and take place before the store opens. CENTER: All-white decor with a large alphabet and caricatures of storybook characters surround thousands of children's books in this large, successful department. Powell's City of Books, Portland, Ore. *BELOW: Le' Bookstore, St. Alberts, Alberta, Canada.*

Children's Bookstore Design

Traditionally, specialty booksellers have been quite good at creating a sense of theater. Most successful children's specialty bookstores have relied on themes such as pageantry, information, or discovery.

The essential children's bookselling environment can be either fantasy-driven or reality-based. In either case, success lies in the store's special message. It must also be well-stocked and have a staff with an exceptional attitude. If a children's bookstore is committed to its market, it will attract customers who desperately want to be part of the scene. Such customers feel good, even virtuous, as they exit better children's bookstore - their arms full of books. We have moved away from those "vanilla" boxes to experiential children's bookstores in which visual merchandise plays an important role. Successful booksellers understand their public's desire to shop in a more exciting environment. The style and design of children's bookstores ranges from contextural to traditional.

Customers' Perceptions and Your Store

Consider customers' perceptions; young mothers and grandmothers alike, in every market, will compare the experience of shopping in a large chain superstore to that of shopping in a specialty store. In a chain superstore there are so many titles it is often impossible to focus. It takes much effort to find the right section, let alone the right book. Many chains aren't fun for children to shop in. On the other hand, specialty children's bookstores, which advertise the stories found in their books in a visually exciting way, are often so appealing that they become an attraction in themselves. Many bookstores beckon children with designs that appeal strongly to the senses. The design of children's stores through the 90s has been characterized by a return to basics and a re-evaluation of the classics. The conspicuous consumption of the 80s has been replaced by a more understated approach. Today's customers select specialty shops they respect and trust. This new consumer attitude is an important consideration for new booksellers and those planning to expand or upgrade their facilities.

Remember the Bottom Line

At the same time, a children's bookstore is a business. Sidelines that are tasteful and related to the total merchandise program, should be considered and integrated into the shelves with concern for their presentation and their "fit". In the past the proliferation of malls, full of stores without strong bookstore market positioning, created successful sales environments, often in spite of themselves. But as more stores were built and as people became educated in the art of consumption, they began to favor those children's booksellers who did a better job of presentation.

Market Separation/Differentiation

As many children's booksellers seek unique personalities for their stores, they are moving away from rigid supermarket or stationery store looks, and similar environments, to quality retail settings. In this chapter we illustrate highly defined traditional and heraldic designs where one would expect to find quality children's books. We also illustrate, in the case of UBS Kid's, a store that provides a new approach to retailing children's books. It is a bookseller's version of The Gap. It is the store's simplicity that is attractive. The store is so clean, the titles so neatly arranged, and the shopping experience so easy, that it encourages customers to buy books.

It takes more than rationality to sell children's books in this increasingly complex, saturated market. Emotional and visual appeals are the key to success. And by continually employing children's senses you can help develop their awareness. As the new millennium approaches, children's book retailing is maturing.

That's because good booksellers are realizing that good store design is the beginning of good customer service. Store design is one of the tools salespeople need to help the customer enjoy shopping. In the sales area, for example, seating may be required, be it a rocker, a straight chair, a children's armchair, bench, step stool or beanbag chair. The number one requirement is to make the store convenient for customers. Number two is to make the store convenient for the salespeople. Everyone who works for and with a specialty children's bookstore has a single job; make sure customers enjoy their time in the store.

Designing Children's Bookstores that Merchandise Customer Service as Well as Products

The children's bookstores and departments we design generally don't resemble one another. Different locations serve different people who shop with different expectations. Our individual designs play to the experience of local customers.

The floor plans focus on visibility, sight-line, and orientation for customers. Customers must be able to see everything clearly so they can move freely from one section to another. It is our theory that, even in the smallest store, if you get people to the back wall they will buy.

Lighting can also help this back-wall strategy. Large specialty stores and superstores grow dark or shadowy along the back wall. In most of our stores a continuous light band rings the walls, adding interest and highlighting to the section signs, customized architectural and design accents, and displays. In large children's superstores, our customers always know where they are.

An example of a store's services might be the offering of better, faster special-order service or gift wrapping. The message is: stay, enjoy yourself, let us take care of everything for you.

Carpet-covered cubes for climbing and the "Red Balloon" storytelling program, low sale tables, and easily accessible wall presentation in the children's book department. Charlesbank Bookshops & Cafe', Boston, Mass.

GAMES-WORKBOOKS

COGNITIVE

LEFT: A medieval theme - suggesting a fantasy land complete with dark green floor, painted blue-green walls and ceiling, stenciled borders, and custom-made flags - was designed to relate the children's books and merchandise sidelines to the imaginations of the customers who shop and enjoy this store. Earthling Bookstore, Santa Barbara, Calif. ABOVE: Victorian details - brass lighting fixtures, fretwork light cornices, pattern ceiling, and case work - were incorporated into the design of this shop. White walls and case work are framed with a lighted sign box and column wall cases made of red oak. This lovely book boutique adds to the appeal of the general book department. James Lundberg Bookstore, Ferris State University, Big Rapids, Mich.

Three-dimensional mama, papa and children bears sit between castles and balance children's books and sideline displays. Webster's Books, Lansing, Mich. *ABOVE R: Green floor and violet fixtures are set against walls with bright accents. CENTER R: Regional signage wall graphics, shaped end panels and "see-through" fixtures.* Webster's Books, Ann Arbor, Mich. *BELOW R: Step display gondolas surround storytelling and play area with antique school benches and tables.* Webster's Books, Lansing, Mich.

ABOVE: *This bookstore and coffee house features a castle where little ones sit on thrones, surrounded by paintings of a multicultural court of noble figures from the past, and read of giants, kittens, knights or space ships. The store provides a space for enchantment - myths, legends, fairy tales and serenity. One of the varied "Sunday at the Castle" programs invited Teddy Bears to accompany their owners to hear stories of familiar bears. Honey and a "little something" were served in this children's Never-Never Land.* Canterbury Booksellers Coffeehouse, Madison, Wis. RIGHT: *Treated as a separate shop, "Place' Pooh" is a small, charming children's book department built on two levels. The main floor is wood, the upper level carpeted, and the shop has many fascinating bookselling symbols and features - low sale tables, gondolas with roof book displays, weather vanes, Captain Hook's brass parrot cage, and a two-level play-house to explore. Framed prints and posters were featured when the shop opened. A scenic art mural was painted for the wall and a custom flag sewn to float over the space.* University of Toronto Book Room, Toronto, Canada.

Another example: some large stores have introduced nursing areas or mother's rooms in women's lounges. In other stores, both women's and men's lounges feature changing tables with diaper dispensers. The whole family is welcome at a quality children's specialty bookstore (see Chapter 3).

We have even found a way to redesign the rest rooms to meet a specialty children's bookstore customer's needs. Our new stores have larger rest rooms. The management of some stores found women were reluctant to leave children in strollers outside the rest room. If they had to use the rest room before they finished shopping they would often go home. When wider doors in rest rooms were introduced for people with disabilities, we discovered they were also an amenity for parents, who could take strollers right into the rest room. Customers who stay in the store - shop in the store - and we love them for it.

These things are often taken for granted. But, we think they enhance the service and convenience of a store. This isn't a grand scheme of our own. It's a notion derived from years of developing plans and designs that attend to customer's concerns.

Children's Bookstore Category Lists

One of our favorite category lists can be found in Table 6.1, shows a lot of imagination and originality for a highly successful (400 - 1,000 SF) store. Included in this list of interesting and fanciful sections are the sidelines and store services offered. It is important that space be provided in this type of specialty shop for children's events, author signings, and storytelling.

Table 6.1 Small Children's Bookshop Category, Sideline,
and Service Listing (400-1,000 square feet)

Main Sections:

ABC/123	Look & Listen
Active Readers	Mysteries & Adventures
Animals	Once Upon a Time
Arts & Crafts	Preschool
Audio	Puzzles
Cards/Wrapping	Rhymes, Songs, & Poems
Children's Classics	Scare Me!
Dinosaurs	Science
First Experiences	Science/Space
Games & Activities	Storybooks/Picturebooks
I'm Reading!	Things That Go
Kidding Around	Things To Do
Laughs & Giggles	Travel Guides
Local Authors	Maps

Sidelines: Rubber stamps, greeting cards, bookmarks, plush.

Services: Gift wrapping, special orders, mail order.

Assuming there is a market adequate to support the sales plan, the list of categories will determine the physical size of the store and its location.

Following is an example of a category list for a large children's specialty bookstore.

ABOVE: Contextural design features, eclectic fixtures, dark background and an imaginative, high build-up table display. The walk-around central service desk and cashier station is conveniently set up. ABOVE R: Books on cassette and Easy Readers sections in this first-rate shop. Harry W. Schwartz Children's Bookshop, Milwaukee, Wis.

Table 6.2   Large Children's Bookshop Category, Sideline, and Service Listing (1,500-2,500 square feet)

Main Sections:

Activity	Ladybird Books
Arts & Crafts	Laughs & Giggles
Audio - Books on Tape	Lift & Look
Babysitters' Club	Nancy Drew & Hardy Boys
Beatrix Potter	Newbery Award Winners
Berenstein Bears	Paperback Picture Books
Beginning Readers	Parenting
Board Books	Picture Books
Bright & Early (Dr. Seuss)	Poetry
Caldecott Award Winners	Pop-Ups
Children's Dictionaries	Pre-School
& Encyclopedias	Religion
Classics	Series - Dell, Yearling, etc.
Color/Activity	Sesame Street
Dinosaurs	Sports
Educational Games	Teacher's Helper
Ethnic Books	Things That Go
Eyewitness Books	Things To Do
Favorite Authors	Travel Guides (Children's)
Favorite Characters	Walt Disney
Favorite Series	Workbooks
Foreign Language	Workbooks/Flashcards
Growing Up	Young Naturalist
History	Young Readers
	Young Scientist

Sidelines: Children's videos, greeting cards, framed prints and posters, balloons, kites, stick-ons, rubber stamps, magnets, puppets, educational toys and computers, table-top games, plush toys, novelty, and clothing.

Services: Gift wrapping, special orders, catalogue, newsletter, mail order, storytelling, author readings, and signings.

The children's book department in this friendly shop delights children and adults alike. Publisher James Lawrence's original ideas work together to capture the gentle humor and other qualities of Beatrix Potter's twenty-three little books and Mother Goose. Pigling Bland sits atop a weather vane and Peter Rabbit waits at attention, paws up, in a nest above a cube between four sales gondolas and tables. And there is a large tree stump, hand-made of copper, that reaches up to the ceiling. A copper owl peeks out of a branch knot in the tree stump. The tree is a place for tikes to explore and is large enough for mom and a couple of kids to sit in, read, and tell stories. The Beatrix Potter-inspired decor - the hare, the copper pig weather vane, and the tree stump - reinforces the quality image of this magical shop. Chapters Books & Cafe', Jelly Mill Shopping Center, Shelburne, Vt.

UBS Kids is a 4,000-square-foot super children's bookstore that now stocks 18,000 titles ... and growing. ABOVE L: Green neon and pictograms designate key title areas. Movable, lighted pocket displays have been provided for work and activity books. Case work is all white with primary color accents. ABOVE R: Main service cash desk is provided with four POS stations. Lighting coves, edged with accent colors, emit soft, indirect lighting. Flex space in front of the desk is used for story-telling, demonstrations and singalongs. CENTER R: Customer information and special order desk is made in primary colors. CD-ROM computer and POS terminals help the staff to help customers. A lighted "Bucky the Badger" reigns overhead. BELOW R: Wide aisles make it easy to shop the comprehensive inventory of the parenting section. BELOW L: Color-keyed focal points, inspired by Superman themes, encourage browsing. UBS Kids, Madison, Wis.

Like The Gap, UBS Kids takes a new approach to retailing. It is the simplicity that provides the attraction. The store is so clean, the titles and sidelines so neatly arranged, and the shopping experience so easy, that it encourages customers to stop, shop and buy books. The image says, "Shop UBS Kids and belong to a group that knows about good children's books and about style."

ABOVE L: Children's music and popular video programs (for sale, of course) are played on two ceiling-mounted monitors. A "train" fixture large enough for four children sports a sign reading POPPY'S EXPRESS, and an electric clock on its nose. New mothers love the wide main aisle, which can accommodate two twin buggies, side by side. ABOVE R: Blue focal point highlights demonstration computers and software display. Step stools are for little people to reach the machines. CENTER L: An exceptional selection of games and toys is coordinated into the merchandising plan with red pictograms and metal wire crib gondola fixtures. BELOW R: The baby and children's clothing department focal point and graphics are well lighted and painted fire engine red. Simple, tasteful fixtures are white.

LEFT: White walls are trimmed with bands of blue turquoise and orange. Peaked feature wall cases bring extra impact to the children's department. ABOVE R: Neat, simple, very workable step displays surround a service desk at the entrance of the "L"-shaped department. LIBERTIES *Fine Books & Music*, Boca Raton, Fla.

CHAPTER 7

BOOKSTORE FIXTURES

Carefully designed and thoughtfully selected bookstore fixtures can make an important contribution to the overall image of a bookstore. The best bookstore fixtures make it easy to show and sell a lot of books.

Store fixtures are an integral element in the design of bookstore space, because they affect merchandise functions such as stacked, face-out, and spine-out book displays. Store fixtures also personalize a store. Fixtures reflect individual preferences, activities, and needs. Successful bookstores require fixtures that make the transition between the shopper, the books, and the services provided by the store.

Store Fixture Types

Fixtures can be freestanding or built in as an integral part of the interior structure. Some units are so well integrated into the architectural design that they become dominant design elements as well as functional pieces. It may even be difficult to distinguish the fixture from the building.

Store fixtures can vary in form from linear or planar to cubic. The lines of a store can be curvilinear, rectilinear, angular, geometric, or free flowing. Proportions can be horizontal or vertical, solid and sturdy, or light and airy. Finishes can have a wide variety of appearances: slick, shiny, warm, soft, rough, heavy, multicolored, or monochromatic.

The countless varieties of store fixtures available today are best classified by use rather than by style or materials. Each of the many different types of bookstore fixtures that we originate, modify, or enhance has a functional merchandising purpose. New fixtures are continually being designed to accommodate greater capacity and to provide a better view of the products. Fixtures are designed to make the titles being presented more attractive, appealing, and available to customers. A checklist of the typical fixtures used to equip a general bookstore can be found in Table 7.1.

Task Units: Cash, Service, and Information Fixtures

Service and information desks can vary as much in function as in style. The selection of a service desk is dependent on the store's needs. Service desk requirements can range from a simple work surface to a multipurpose unit used for cashiers, special orders, information, storage, and gift wrapping.

Freestanding information desks can take the form a *U,* an *L,* or a straight table. The traditional service desk of the past consisted of a writing surface, space for a

Skylight over full-vision, glass front, and movable glass doors, provide easy access and reinforce visual merchandise presentation on two levels. RIT Bookstore, Rochester, N.Y.

cash drawer or cash register, and cabinets below for the storage of bags, books, and supplies. Today, service information units are available with handicap cashier stations and access panels for the installation of electric gear, computers, telephones, and modems. Usually, these desks are provided with at least one drawer and adjustable bag shelves. Often, there is also an L-shaped extension that can provide a secondary work surface or space for a typewriter or computer with a keyboard and cathode ray tube.

Specialized Store Fixtures

Independent bookstore design often calls for specialized fixtures. Many of these specialized units are tailored specifically for one particular store. They are designed to meet a specific merchandising objective. There are, for example, fixtures made especially for remainder and hurt books, tiered pocket units for children's books, soft-bound manuals, crossword puzzles, and atlases, and special units with a greater number of pockets for magazines.

Special service desks, tables, and stands are made to accommodate computers, keyboards, and printers. Storage units are also customized for computers and their supporting hardware and software.

Many bookstores use residential furniture modified for retail use, as well as furnishings and accessories common to residential use.

Featured Fixture Design

Bookstore sales fixtures should be as simple as possible, because they are merely a means to an end. When basic fixtures become overly elaborate, they dominate the product display and detract from its sales appeal. On the other hand, featured decorative pieces can serve the purpose of immediately attracting interest.

ABOVE: *Focal point display with castered, pocketed merchandiser for oversized children's activity books, board books and chalk and tack boards.* UBS Kids, Madison, Wis.

Table 7.1 Checklist of Bookstore Fixture Types	
• Wall Cases	• Show Window Back Wall Cases
• Gondolas	• Sale Table Risers
• Children's Specialty Gondolas	• Light Cornices
• Step Stools	• Column Enclosures
• Dictionary Tables	• Corner Fillers
• Inserts (Kids')	• Audio Cassette Displays
• Inserts (Maps)	• Newspaper and Magazine Racks
• Whales	• Folded-Map Racks
• Sale Tables	• Acrylic Easels and Holders
• Cash Wrap Counters	• Roll-Map Units
• Information/Special Order Desks	• Globe Displays

Scale and Size

Store fixtures are manufactured in many sizes and proportions. Selections should be made not only on the basis of use and function, but also on the basis of the space available, purpose, capacity, proportion to the overall environment, and scale with the people who will use them.

Some store fixtures may seem visually scaled to a space, but may be too small to present an adequate book display. Some fixtures might also seem appropriate because of their dimensions, but their visual scale may not work in harmony with the space. For example, wall cases selected for customers' browsing use might be very attractive, but out of scale and context with other details throughout the store. Or, a very large gondola might seem to overpower its targeted shoppers.

Quality of Fixture Construction

Craftsmanship and durability are important qualities to look for when buying store fixtures. Try to be sure that high-quality materials and sound construction methods have been used. Since much of store fixture construction is concealed, it is important to be aware of the reputations of various products and manufacturers who provide them.

Durability

The durability of a store fixture depends not only on its construction and materials, but also on its intended use. Fixtures should be well built, but they do not necessarily have to be indestructible. Fixtures that will be moved frequently should be mounted on casters. They will then be easier to move and their life will be extended, because they were built to be durable for their intended use. Construction of mobile fixtures should be stout to withstand being moved when full of stock weighing 1,000 or more pounds.

Many of the stores that we designed and built twenty years ago are still functional and attractive. This is largely because their fixtures were carefully chosen on the basis of their intended use.

Theme tables with stacker boxes and end merchandising panels create a dynamic bookselling environment. Southern Oregon State College Bookstore.

Modular Store Fixture Systems

For economy and practicality, bookstore fixtures should all be the same module size. Same-sized modules permit the interchanging of shelves and inserts for children's flats, atlases, maps, art books, and pamphlets. Interchangeable hang-bars, crossbars, face-out displays, and drawer cabinets used for sidelines can also be changed from one store fixture to the next. The use of standard module dimensions reduces the number of spare shelves and other parts required, and also simplifies their storage. It allows your staff to move entire sections and departments from one area to another with ease. Modular fixtures require less initial investment than nonstandard fixtures, are adaptable to a greater variety of merchandising shifts, and will better contribute to the order and atmosphere of your bookstore.

Life-Cycle Costs

The initial expense of store fixtures is only one aspect of their cost. Life-cycle costs, including maintenance expenses for the expected life of fixtures and their replacement costs, also must be considered. Maintenance includes cleaning, repairing, and refinishing. Cleaning entails vacuuming, stain removal, and the waxing or protecting of feature display units.

A budget might provide for the initial acquisition and installation of store fixtures, but life-cycle costs might outweigh the funds available to maintain the units. It is usually better to invest more money initially for quality fixtures that will

ABOVE: Custom, limited-editions cases with adjustable shelves and locked glass doors. LIBERTIES, Boca Raton, Fla. BELOW: Greeting card fixtures. Webster's Books, Lansing, Mich.

not require as much expenditure over their expected life as will fixtures of a lesser quality. Selections must be balanced to obtain the best quality for the best price. However, available money may limit the selection. We might then recommend less expensive items for some areas and better quality fixtures for prime locations, where extended use and image are particularly important.

Store Fixture Materials and Construction

Many specialty materials are used to fabricate and assemble the components of the different types of store fixtures required by independent bookstores. Some of the most commonly used materials and their applications are described below.

Wood. Solid woods, veneers, and composite wood products are most frequently used in fabricating bookstore fixtures. There are, of course, numerous species of softwood and hardwood. When natural wood fixtures are required, oak, walnut, and mahogany are most often used. Poplar (white wood), sugar pine, birch, and maple are close-grained woods suitable for stain, lacquer, enamel, and paint finishes. Pine and poplar woods, available in long lengths, are often used by fabricators for molding, trim, and cornice work.

Plywood. Plywood is a versatile, layered wood product available in flat sheets and curved shapes. Plywood derives its great strength from alternating the layers at right angles to one another, which produces strength in two directions. Metal, laminate, and other wood-surface materials can be bonded to plywood. Cabinet-grade plywood is strong, durable, and available with fireproofed qualities. Close-grained plywood can be readily stained, painted, or laminated with plastic veneers. Plywood is most often used for shelves, where strength is required, and for case ends, drawer fronts, and entire bookstore fixtures where strength and durability are needed for heavy wear and tear.

Composite Wood Panels. Medium-density fiberboard (MDF), a substitute for plywood panels, has gained universal acceptance in the furniture and fixture industry. MDF is reasonably priced, hard, and readily accepts paint, lacquer, or laminate finishes. MDF is more stable and less inclined to warp than plywood, particularly if plastic laminate is applied to one side. On the other hand, MDF has little strength to resist bending. Shelves made of MDF alone will develop a permanent sag under the weight of dictionaries, atlases, and other heavy books. However, with proper reinforcement, MDF shelves can be quite serviceable and can reduce your total fixture costs.

Metal. Metal is used for complete fixture systems and shelf components. We have found that thin, strong, and durable metal bookshelves are particularly suitable for textbook stocking. Painted an appropriate color, metal shelves blend into book-jacket colors and disappear. Slotted, chrome-plated metal tubing is versatile and suitable for many bookstore applications. Assembled with snap-together fastenings, slotted tubing can be used to make show-window etageres, gift and stationery towers, book build-ups, and soft goods displays. Metal grid display systems provide an alternative to wood slatwall.

Metal-Faced Panels. Large, thin sheets of stainless steel, aluminum, brass, and bronze, with polished or brushed finishes, can be laminated to MDF or plywood. These sheets are useful for fabricating fixture accents. Properly used, metal accents can enhance the aesthetic qualities of certain specialty bookstore display fixtures and lift the store ambiance.

Glass. Glass is used for shelves, in showcases, and in the hinged and sliding doors of limited editions bookcases. Tempered glass is the quality best used for bookstore fixtures, show windows, view windows, and glazed doors. Laminated glass is an alternative to tempered glass, and is particularly useful for skylights, partition walls, and security-cabinet fixture work where the edges of the glass are protected from view. Plate glass mirrors are found in elegant bookstore design and fixture work. Glass mirrors can visually reduce the size of columns, expand the size of small spaces, and be useful for security purposes.

Plastic Laminates. High-pressure plastic laminates and melamine surfaces are used for store fixture surfaces. These are very durable materials and are available in many different colors, textures, and patterns. Plastic laminates are impervious to most cleaners and are easy to maintain. Originally made only in a 1/16-inch thickness for countertop use, both 1/16-inch and 1/32-inch thick vertical grade laminates are available today. Vertical grade laminate may be successfully applied to sheetrock (gypsum wall board) and plaster surfaces or bonded to plywood, MDF, and other high-quality particle-board cores. Panel sizes range up to 5 feet wide and 12 feet long.

Plexiglas, Lucite, and Acrylic Plastics. Tough, hard, and transparent acrylic, Plexiglas, and Lucite plastic sheets, shapes, and rods are available in a variety of sizes and thicknesses. These materials are relatively easy to cut, drill, heat-form and bend. Category sign holders and book easels, greeting card trays, display cube steps and risers, transparent apparel cubes, and counter bases are often fabricated with acrylic sheeting.

Colorful moulded plastic tables and stackable bookshelves are ranked the best for show window props. Plastic storage bins and cubes, door pulls, hinges, and other hardware are also available for use in store fixture fabrication. Waterproofed and flame-retardant plastic upholstery is used for bookstore chairs and window seats. Vinyl wall covering is also sometimes used in bookstore finishing and fixture work.

ABOVE: See-through type large format book and calendar merchandiser. Webster's Books, Lansing, Mich. *BELOW: Special gondola insert for sheet music.* LIBERTIES Fine Books & Music, Boca Raton, Fla.

Fixture Flexibility and Adaptability

For most bookstores, flexibility is important. The ability to convert a merchandise arrangement from Business Books to Clip Art Books, for example, requires that the fixtures be flexible and adaptable. Flexibility in the adjustment of shelves' height and depth is particularly important.

Adjustable Shelves. The best adjustable bookshelves are suspended from their ends. End suspension prevents damage to book jackets caused by shelf supports located midway along the underside of the shelf. Adjustable, angled, and flat supply department shelves also are supported from the back at each end. Individual wood and glass adjustable shelves for non-book items are also supported from the back and mounted on adjustable knife brackets supported by a metal standard, fixed to the back of the store fixture, or to a finished wall of the store.

Display Inserts. Stepped and pocketed display inserts for children's and art books, periodicals, outlines, memo books, graph paper, and monographs can be added to achieve almost total flexibility; they can be as simple, economical, and attractive as you choose. Snap-on formed wire displays for video and computer program display are economical and effective.

Power and Signal Wiring. The age of electronics has made a major impact on point-of-sale bookstore fixture design. Provision must be made to facilitate the wiring of computer terminals, cash registers, CD-ROMs, computers, telephones, modems, faxes, calculators, typewriters, and other business machines. The tops and backs of cash wraps and information desks must be designed and fabricated to permit wires from these electronic items to connect with power and signal box outlets located in the base of store fixtures.

Access Panels. Access panels are needed in the floor of cash wraps to expose the space below the bottom of cash wraps to view. They are also necessary to make room for technicians to install and connect wiring and cabling for the electronic equipment your store will need - today and tomorrow.

Hangware. Hang rods and crossbars, adaptable for waterfall face-out bracket highlighting, can be installed in case work and on slatwall. This type of display fixture is used in travel bookstores to market T-shirts, backpacks, maps, posters,

ABOVE: Face-out, lighted magaazine section and end-cap merchandise. BELOW: Wall and column treatment. Biola University Bookstore, La Mirada, Calif.

and related products. Other bookstores use metal standards with brackets to support wire-grid insert panels and cornice lighting equipment.

Reusing, Refinishing, and Remodeling Store Fixtures

It would be ideal for everyone if we could begin planning every bookstore from scratch. For many booksellers, however, that will not be the case. You might buy an existing bookstore business and, for practical reasons, have us reposition existing wood store fixtures and accessories into a new store image. We do this kind of remodeling fairly regularly. While replanning and reimaging a store with a great deal of existing equipment is often difficult and complex, most existing fixtures can be successfully blended into a new plan and a new store image. We get a lot of satisfaction from transforming a tired, disorganized, and dowdy sales area into one that is smart, upbeat, warm, friendly, and profitable.

Techniques of Store Fixture Refinishing

If existing fixtures are made of metal, they can be refinished with an electrostatic paint finish technique. An eclectic collection of wood fixtures can all be painted one color or antiqued with one of many kits available. Counters can be cut down or added to and a new laminate applied to worn and scratched top surfaces. Chipped and scratched glass showcase tops and shelves are easy to replace.

It is certainly possible to obtain a fresh, new image by refinishing old fixtures and rearranging them in an imaginative new plan. However, the cost of labor is sometimes so high that the expense of a renovated store fixture is nearly as much as replacing it with a new one. Each store situation is different and must be studied and analyzed to determine, *before starting*, the practicality of moving and refinishing existing equipment.

Great Looking Stores Don't Have to Come at Great Cost

Here are some tips to bear in mind when selecting fixtures.
- Consider the function or purpose of the fixture. Will it be moved? Does it need casters? Must it be adjustable? Is it adaptable to more than one category of books or merchandise? What finishes are available? Is there an up-charge for colors?
- Consider the fixture from a merchandising point of view. Will the fixture expand your creative options? Should it be lighted? Does it require special signage? How will it be attached? What are its dimensions?
- Keep an open mind. Chrome and glass etageres make wonderful window and tower merchandisers, but so do colorful plastic milk crates and wood boxes.
- Before you buy mass-produced fixtures, check the sizes, materials, and construction methods used. Turn the fixture over. One look at the bottom and back will tell a lot. Where are the access panels? Are the shelves adjustable? How will computer and terminal connections be wired? How are the drawers mounted?
- Think about maintenance. How long do you expect these fixtures to last? How long is your lease?
- Don't limit your merchandising plan to one style of fixture. Good design cuts across style boundaries. A mixture of styles gives the bookstore scheme variety and a unique touch. An unusual breakfront, exceptional chairs at a browsing table, a stained glass insert, or a grandfather clock can become a decorative tour de force.
- Don't overspend and over-equip. Ask our advice - and take it.
- Unless there is a valid reason not to, always buy new store fixtures delivered and installed directly from store fixture manufacturers. Avoid buying store fixtures from distributors and wholesalers who will buy them at about the same price available to you but add a significant mark-up for handling the transaction.

- If you are on a shoestring budget to open your first store, or if your shop needs a makeover and funds are low, don't resign yourself to shabbiness and dreams of "someday." Think about color.
- Have you considered used fixtures? For a variety of reasons, booksellers advertise bookstore fixtures for sale - most made by the popular store fixture vendors - in just about every issue of *Publishers Weekly* and *The American Bookseller.*
- Industry magazines also are a good place to find good buys in previous-owner merchandise systems, as well as office and back room equipment.

Sources of Equipment

Industry publications list advertisers who make several grades of bookstore fixtures. From these firms, you can obtain catalogs from which you can order one fixture or an entire store. If you have not actually seen the equipment that you want to order, ask for the name of stores in your area that have bought and use fixtures made by the company you are considering. Go see them. Quality and production control are two of the store fixture industry's major headaches. Nothing is more frustrating than to receive a long-awaited store fixture, only to find that it does not meet your expectations. Working together, we can arrange for the procurement of your store fixture needs from a manufacturer you can trust to be on time with the quality product you need and the cost to meet your budget. KWA does not make or sell store fixtures. By this process, however, we can reduce the uncertainty and make the purchase, delivery, and installation of fixtures less of an ordeal for you.

Ordering Bookstore Fixtures

Order store fixtures as far in advance as possible. Long delivery time is a fact of life in retailing. Bookstore fixtures have a delivery period that varies from 3 to 8 weeks after the order is placed. During the late summer, when most stores are remodeled, you can expect the delivery period to be as long as 10 to 12 weeks. The best way to design your new store is for us to estimate your needs, develop your plans, design the store, and order early (see Appendix II).

Guarantees and Warranties

Manufacturers of store fixtures, furniture, carpet, and other products used for bookstore furnishings provide a guarantee or warranty that their merchandise will perform and last for a specified period of time, generally one year. *Guarantee* and *warranty* are often used interchangeably, but some federal and state laws do specify a difference. Some manufacturers will provide promises as a limited warranty for a part of a product. Some warranties are implied or understood, such as that an adjustable product obviously must be adjustable. Warranty and guarantee programs can help ascertain how reliable a product is, particularly if the covered periods are longer than usual.

Contextural design treatment of column using four sides of shelving and theme table positioned for maximum visual merchandising use. Webster's Books, Ann Arbor, Mich.

CHAPTER 8

COLOR AND LIGHTING DESIGN

Color and light are two of the most important elements in bookstore design. Color values and color composition accent, highlight, and identify book categories and merchandise displays in retail settings. Color can be used to establish the visual proportions of the sales space, and to reinforce the psychological character of the store. Color is the element that contributes most to a sense of visual unity in the bookstore front and interior design. As with every other aspect of bookselling, successful color coordination depends on careful planning and professional know-how.

Image and Recognition

Image and recognition can be incorporated into any bookstore through its color scheme. We believe that the color scheme for each bookstore should be customized - that each be unique and effective, and easy to remember for the book customers who rush from mall to mall and from store to store. To set our store apart, our color scheme should be unique in its selection and should strongly contribute to the overall ambiance.

Over the years, we have observed how dull and repetitious most chain and many independent bookstores really are. Booksellers are generally not quick to make changes or to take chances, or to try imaginative retail design approaches to color. Quality independent bookstores are viewed by many customers as institutions. That is partially true. Some are institutions. Bookstores do present some degree of stability and security in the community. But if we are not careful, that stability and security can translate into blandness and dullness. There is a very real need for originality, excitement, and distinctness in bookstores of this generation.

Color in Merchandising

Many new bookstores incorporate color schemes that portray a richness and style that is more personal and inviting than those of the past. These new color schemes have set aside the pristine beauty of the pared down minimalistic look of the past decade, in favor of color schemes that echo times past, from Victorian to Regency to modern eras.

The background colors of wall and store fixtures should be either quiet and in harmony with stronger merchandise colors, to successfully accent book-jacket

Wood beams with raised coffers, recessed down lights and brass lanterns set the tone for this English Georgian inspired interior. The superior materials - fine wood floors, ceramic tile aisles, oak trim and cabinets, mirrors and plants - reflect the quality of the book collection. Charlesbank Bookshops & Cafe', Boston, Mass.

colors, or of a color value that complements the merchandise. A warm beige background works nicely with the colorful book-jackets of a cookbook section, while a deep plum or navy blue background contrasts well with the display of predominantly white papeteries in a stationery and supply department.

The impression of color that we get from a retail store setting comes from more than the paint color of the walls. The color, texture, and finish of each building material, graphic, and store fixture exposed to view must be selected, coordinated, and specified to harmonize with the PDM strategy, image, and design of the new bookstore.

Color Selection

There are several ways to approach color selection. Let us describe the way we do it. Following the finalization of the PDM Spec, our designers select and coordinate several color schemes in harmony with the character and image of your new bookstore. These color schemes are presented to you for your concurrence and approval.

Color Harmony

A color scheme that harmonizes throughout a bookstore provides an integrated visual experience and a feeling of comfort. A bookstore in which every department has a completely different color scheme can create a jumpy feeling. An integrated color scheme ties together all of the departments and visual elements of the store into one harmonious composition.

Color and Artificial Light

In the choice of color, a great deal depends on the bookstore's setting. Bookstores located inside an arcade-enclosed mall or a student union building may require more intense, dramatic color schemes. Bookstores in these settings depend on artificial illumination, which can be controlled, and this influences the selection of color schemes. Artificial light often plays odd tricks with colors. Historical, children's, mystery, design, science fiction, or specialty bookshops and departments that are artificially illuminated can easily carry off more dramatic finishes and color schemes, because they are expected by their customers, who enjoy these special effects.

Natural and artificial light illuminate this three sided map display. Gettysburg Visitors Center, Gettysburg, Pa.

Color and Sunlight

Bookstores with large exterior window areas have another problem - and blessing: sunlight! The exposure of major glass areas makes a critical impact on the selection and application of interior color. The possibility and extent of color distortions and reflections on windows, books, and merchandise caused by sunlight during certain daylight hours is a factor that must be taken into account and reckoned with.

Here are some basic rules we use. Avoid a cold blue, green, or violet in a shop with windows facing north. Do not use an intense red-orange or yellow in a shop that faces west. If the bookstore is flooded with sunshine through show windows or a skylight for part of the day, a bright, high-intensity color scheme would be distracting. If, on the other hand, yours is a commodious light-filled bookstore with wood fixtures, high ceilings, and windows that face north, use colors that are warm, cheerful, and stimulating - colors that create a sense of intimacy.

Use of Color to Compensate for Scale and Proportions

- If a shop is big and open, dark-toned walls will tend to make the room seem smaller and more friendly.

- Greater visual depth in a department can be accomplished by painting one wall a bright, warm color and the other three walls a lighter color.

- Colors expand when they reflect light, and make objects seem larger, more spacious, and more cheerful.

Painted Ceilings

Most painted ceilings are finished the same color (beige or white) as the walls in bookstores. Height can be added to the ceiling by painting it a lighter color than the walls.

To achieve a balanced color perspective, a general rule is to paint ceilings three shades lighter than wall colors. There are, however, exceptions to this rule. Painting the ceiling a darker value tends to make it disappear. In a very small, low-ceilinged room, a dark ceiling sometimes works out well.

Conceptualizing Color Schemes

A variety of illusions can be produced by the imaginative use of color accents and graphics. But these things are tricky and should be left in the hands of a designer with considerable knowledge and experience in the design of bookstore color schemes.

Color schemes do not have to be complex to be successful and unique. Most bookstore color schemes need surprisingly few paint colors, since so many colors are predetermined by the books themselves, by the carpet, tile, or wood floors, and by the finish of the store fixtures and the textures and shades of metal, stone, or other building materials used in the structure of the store. The most interesting bookstore color schemes utilize five colors or less.

Our designers create color concepts that seem fresh and new to the shopper by keeping the major color area of the store neutral and selecting colors from among the most neutral to the most brilliant hues for accents. Sharp accent colors can be used, but with discretion. Secondary areas, which include store fixtures and window treatments, can utilize more intense color combinations to create an overall ambiance that sets a specialty section within the store apart.

This approach to color offers an immediate point of reference to popular decorating styles. We find that this approach can generate the most successful schemes, those that are both safe and easy to follow.

Painted ceiling, neutral walls and tile floor, accent carpet, graphic panel, fixturing and lighted magazine display. Dietrick VPI C-Store, Blacksburg, Va.

Color Terms

There are numerous good books that deal with the science of color and its theory of application. For our purpose, we will simplify some of the common terms that deal with the properties of color.

Hue and Tint. Color is grouped into three families. A *hue* is a single color, such as a red, yellow, or blue, in all its lighter and darker variations. Any hue diluted with white is called a *tint*. If, for instance, the primary color yellow is diluted with white, a lighter color, a yellow tint, is the result.

Shade. A *shade* is any hue mixed with gray to darken it, except in the case of wood stain. Stains are grayed to begin with. Clear thinner is usually used to lighten them. So we would say, ''It is a lighter or darker shade of natural wood stain color.''

Intensity and Chroma. A value of painted or printed color refers to its light or dark color intensity. The *intensity* of a color refers to the color's purity, that is, the degree of brightness or dullness of a particular color. Another term used interchangeably with intensity is *chroma*.

Neutral, Warm, and Cool Colors. Neutral colors are black, white, and gray, all metallics, and also tints and shades of colors, such as beige, which are predominantly gray or brown in cast. Warm colors are red, yellow, and orange. Cool colors

ABOVE: Multicolored scheme features bold accent colors, banding the cove lighting details. UBS Kids, Madison, Wis.
RIGHT: Color-corrected, long-lasting, metal halide lighting is effective in high ceiling spaces. Minnesota Book Center, University of Minnesota, Minneapolis, Minn.

are blue, green, and purple or violet. With the addition of gray to any color, its intensity is lowered and it becomes duller.

Chroma. The *chroma*, or intensity, of a color also helps to determine where and how to use it. Strong colors or those of high intensity are best used in small areas, such as graphic panels, and as accent colors. Deep shades of a color can give a book department either richness and warmth, or a weighty feeling if they are not relieved by tints.

Multi-Color Schemes. Stimulating bookstore color schemes that alternate between light and dark, dull and bright, or matte and reflective values and surfaces are stimulating. Bold and unusual schemes are appropriate in the right setting. The use of gloss finishes on doors and frames, contrasted with a flat wall finish surface, creates a pleasing effect.

Monotone Color Schemes. One hue - say, khaki or gray - can be employed for an entire store by varying the shades and tints, and the cool and warm values of the color on walls, ceilings, and case interiors with materials such as paint, laminate, or vinyl fabric. Monotone color schemes can be extended by using contrasting textures in carpet, floor finishes, and ceiling textures.

Graphics and Accessory Colors. Little things mean a lot in signs, graphics, scenic art, paintings, posters, and other nonstructural objects in the bookstore. These items can be finished with accent colors to legitimately call attention to shelves of merchandise. Bright red, yellow, black and green hues for step stools, bookcarts, chair and stool cushions, directories, posters, paintings, signage, smokers, and accent light fixtures add a nice finishing touch to the bookstore and give a feeling of visual completeness.

Texture. Aficionados who use textures in design and decoration can choose from historic documents to fanciful and more impressionistic interpretations for ideas. *Texture* is the description of the surface of a structural or graphic material in its natural state. A texture may also describe the finish of a material, a carved relief or applied decoration, a woven or tufted fabric, or a composite of several of these materials. Textures are usually thought of as dimensional in character, though rough, smooth, etched, and sandblasted materials, patterned stained glass, and glass mirrors all qualify as textures. Luxurious, mirror-polished brass and coffered ceiling tiles possess texture as much as do rugged, hammered copper or brass.

Textures can be smooth or comfortably rough, as with wood, natural brick, stone, or plaster surfaces. Textures can be soft, pliable, and elegant, with the surface look and feel of suede, rawhide, leather, or fabric. A number of new surface textures in vinyl wall covering and wallpaper, with dimensional texture designs on dull and reflective metallic foil backgrounds, have renewed our designers' interests in these handsome materials.

ABOVE L: Cornice lighting with an eggcrate soffit eliminates glare and view of light bulbs. LIBERTIES, Boca Raton, Fla. ABOVE R: Lighted glass globes hung over the information/special order desk identify it and attract the attention of passers-by. Webster's Books, Lansing, Mich.

Bringing the Bits and Pieces Together

When all the swatches and samples of colors, finishes, and textures, and the bits and pieces of specialty materials have been assembled and agreed upon, they become the color scheme. Smooth color transitions from department to department and from floor to floor are important in achieving a harmonious overall color scheme.

Color Boards. Once it has been determined, color coordination information is formalized in typewritten or large hand-lettered color and finish schedules. The color schedules are made to coordinate the application of bookstore materials with construction process requirements. For convenience and practical use, duplicate samples and swatches of the final selections are applied onto sheets of foam core-board, which instantly become *color boards*.

Several color boards may be required for a large project and are always necessary in planning multi-floor color schemes. With these color boards, one can tell at a glance whether the colors are compatible with the image and character of the bookstore and if they achieve the ambiance desired.

Small duplicate color boards, 8-1/2 by 11 inches, are often made to accompany the color specifications and charts. They are assembled in ring binders and distributed to the fixture contractor, general contractor, and painting contractor for coordination purposes.

Timing and Distribution of Color Schedules

In the implementation phase of a bookstore construction project, the timing, preparation, and distribution of final color and finish information is critical. All color decisions should be finalized during the planning and design stage. Having all the information at hand simplifies the bidding process, allows early ordering, expedites the entire building project, and avoids errors and unnecessary delays.

Light and Color

The perceived color of merchandise or other colors in the store can vary, depending on the type of light source. Ideally, shoppers should be able to look at merchandise under lighting as similar as possible to that where the merchandise will be used. However, this can vary from daylight to incandescent light in the home, and can be any of a number of colors of fluorescent or high-intensity discharge lamps in factories or offices. The best choice is often a good color-rendering source with a moderate color temperature.

The color temperature (chromaticity) of a light source sets the tone of the space and is measured in degrees Kelvin (K). The warmer the color, the lower the degree; the bluer or cooler the color, the higher the degree.

The color-rendering ability of a light source is a measure of how well it makes colored objects appear. This is expressed by the Color Rendering Index (CRI), which is a number representing how color samples appear when compared with a reference light source with the same color temperature. The higher the number, the better the color appearance.

Light Sources

Lighting in bookstores is of two kinds: natural light and artificial light. With both kinds of lighting, numerous options are available to reduce energy demands without sacrificing the quality of light within an interior space.

Natural Light. The greatest source of natural light available to most bookstores is provided by the sun, and it's free! Controlled sunlight is of great value, particularly when it can be designed to penetrate deep into a store through skylights and clerestories.

The quality of sunlight entering the store is affected by the compass orientation of the glassfront and skylight locations. Careful planning and control of sunlight can reduce energy costs and improve the physical and psychological pleasure derived from its use.

Another, more esoteric, source of light in a bookstore comes from natural fireplaces. The flickering flames given off by fireplaces, seen through the window of a bookstore on a cold snowy night, can act as a beacon to welcome and draw

ABOVE: Low-voltage, track-lighting systems provide an effective method of illuminating and bringing out the product colors, wall print and map displays. Gettysburg Visitors Center, Gettysburg, Pa. *RIGHT: Natural daylight and artificial (incandescent) lighting, sourced from track lights and chandeliers, illuminate the customer service desk and cafe'. Wood flooring and fixtures balance the deep blue-green color used on the columns and the ceiling.* Earthling Bookstore, Santa Barbara, Calif.

ABOVE: *Indirect lighting from green glass shades on brass chandeliers and column-mounted wall sconces are the principal sources for illumination. Beige and white floor tile, deep green carpet, cornice and graphics are combined with brass lighting details in this contextural design environment for a scholarly book department.* Appalachian State University Bookstore, Boone, N.C. *ABOVE R: Track lighting is used to create a picture gallery effect in this print poster shop.* RIT Bookstore, Rochester, N.Y.

customers into the store and encourage them to stay longer. Seats around a fireplace are natural focal points, places where people feel welcome, comfortable, and at ease.

Artificial Light. Light brings store interiors to life. It is important to our activities and perceptions of the world around us. By controlling and designing with natural and artificial light, our designers can create striking design concepts in interior spaces, as well as provide for the visual needs of user activities.

A wide range of energy-saving electrical light sources are available to booksellers, and new types of more efficient and miniaturized lighting fixtures and lamps are introduced in a steady stream.

Artificial light is important as a form of design and merchandising. It is similar to the other basic design elements of space, line, form, color, and texture, since it stimulates our perceptions of these elements and creates sales.

Bookstore Lighting Categories

To provide efficient and comprehensive store lighting, three basic categories of retail lighting are needed in a bookstore environment: general, accent, and perimeter. General lighting is needed to provide optimum quantity, distribution, and direction of color to establish overall visibility and ambiance. Accent lighting is needed to add visual impact to displays and to draw shoppers' attention to them. Perimeter lighting is used to draw attention to wall displays, as well as to contribute

to the attractiveness of the store's environment. The level of light used to accent merchandise is usually three to three-and-one-half times as high as that for general circulation areas. For featured displays, the accent lighting level should be four times higher than that for general book sales areas.

The Efficiency Variable

Some light sources convert electricity into light more efficiently than others. Incandescent lamps, for example, although widely used because of their convenience, are the least efficient lamps available for lighting in stores. Fluorescent and high-intensity discharge lamps generally are two to five times more efficient than incandescent lamps. For this reason, fluorescent lighting has been successfully used in store lighting for decades, and high-intensity discharge lamps are now coming into wider usage.

The best fluorescent lamp color for most store lighting applications will be one of the SP or SPX Specification Series types. These lamps provide both high efficiency and good (SP) or very good (SPX) color rendering, because they use rare earth phosphors. SP and SPX lamps eliminate the efficiency trade-off previously necessary to achieve good color rendering. Some of the new, compact BIAX® lamps are available at 2700K. Table 8.1 shows the various characteristics of fluorescent lamps.

ABOVE L: Suspended tube light fixture with accent track lighting lowers the high ceiling and frames this pleasant general book department. ABOVE R: Wall-mounted contextural-shielded, tube-fluorescent lighting adds highlights and shadows to the all-white background of the first floor sales space. DeAnza College Bookstore, Cupertino, Calif.

Color Temperature	Standard Colors	Specifications	Series Colors	Deluxe Colors
Kelvin (K) Approximate	Fair Colors High Efficiency	Good Color High Efficiency	Very Good Color High Efficiency	Excellent Color Fair Efficiency
3000K	Warm White (WW)	SP30	SPX30	Deluxe Warm White (WWX)
3500K		SP35	SPX35	
4100K	Cool White (CW) & Lite White (LW)	SP41	SPX41	Deluxe Cool White (CWX)
5000K				Chroma 50 (C50)
6200K	Daylight (D)			
7500K				Chroma 75 (C75)

Table 8.1 Fluorescent Lamp Characteristics*

* Characteristics based on GE lamps.

The use of alternating pendant and low-voltage, accent, show-window track lighting is a simple, workable approach to POS merchandise lighting. Moody Bookstore, Chicago, Ill.

Lighting Fixture Types and Techniques

The lighting fixtures called the luminaries are the housing for the lamp and are an integral part of a building's electrical system, transforming energy into usable light. Luminaries are available in a variety of shapes and sizes that can determine the shape and direction of the light beam.

Five common types of mounting methods for manufactured luminaries determine the direction of the light beam: recessed, ceiling-mounted, wall-mounted, suspended, and track-mounted.

Fluorescent, incandescent, and high-intensity discharge light sources can be used for retail lighting; however, each has unique characteristics and should be chosen to fit your lighting, merchandising, and economic objectives.

Recessed. Recessed, fluorescent, metal halide, and incandescent luminaries provide direct light. They are mounted above the ceiling line, the bottom generally flush with the ceiling. Recessed luminaries are popular for general lighting and can utilize all types of lamps. They can also be used for accent to highlight wall washing.

Ceiling-Mounted. Ceiling-mounted luminaries produce direct light and are very efficient, impeding neither light nor heat. They are mounted directly on the ceiling and their light beam can be directed in a wide pattern. Installation and revamping are generally easy and relatively inexpensive. Ceiling-mounted luminaries can lower the effective height of a ceiling.

Wall-Mounted. Wall-mounted fixtures, often called *scones*, provide direct, indirect, diffuse, or direct-indirect light. These fixtures are used mainly for decorative purposes and tend to bring down the line of sight in a space with a very high ceiling. On the other hand, if a ceiling is very low, the clearance for passersby may be impeded by a wall-mounted fixture. Some wall-mounted luminaries incorporate a reflector plate against the wall to reflect any lost light and to create a focal point of brightness.

Suspended. Suspended, or pendant, luminaries can produce direct, indirect, diffuse, or direct-indirect light beams. These fixtures are suspended below the ceiling and, depending on the ceiling height, can be adjustable. One major advantage of these fixtures is their appearance: they become lighted ornaments when suspended in an interior space. Large suspended luminaries can also create a canopy effect. Some building codes require large suspended fixtures to have earthquake hangers so the fixtures will sway but not fall in the event of an earthquake or other disaster.

Track-Mounted. Track-mounted luminaries can provide direct, indirect, or direct-indirect light. A track-mounted lighting system consists primarily of two parts: the track and the luminary. This type of lighting system is very popular because it offers optimum flexibility in a vast range of lighting effects and can be economical. The track itself is an electrical raceway that supplies power to the luminaries. The luminaries can be mounted anywhere on the track and moved horizontally or vertically. The track can be surface-mounted, recessed in the ceiling, or attached to a wall, and can have pendant fixtures hanging from it. Track lighting systems come in a variety of sizes and shapes and can be mounted almost anywhere to serve a multitude of purposes.

LEFT: Shaped lighting coves and pull-down accent lighting add to "flexibility" of "flex space" in the F.S.U. James Lundberg Bookstore, Big Rapids, Mich.

Lighting Systems

Spatially-Integrated Lighting System. Spatially-integrated lighting systems can be defined as lighting that is built in and integral to the construction of a bookstore. Light sources in the cove are relatively invisible and can be controlled to enhance the brightness within a space without creating glare in the field of view.

Cove Lighting. Cove lighting is concealed in a continuous trough that is usually paneled and directed toward the ceiling. Coves are a good choice to give a feeling of height or to emphasize cathedral or vaulted ceilings. Cove lighting provides a soft, uniform, nonglaring light and is best used as a supplement to other lighting. Shaped lighting coves are made of plaster or fiberglas.

Cornice Lighting. Cornices are mounted at or near the ceiling and direct light downward, to give books an interesting lighted effect. Cornices are used to conceal the actual light source, to provide a reflected ambient effect for a space, and to display category signs. Cornice lighting is usually made of wood products.

Soffit Lighting. Soffit lighting is often used in a dropped or furred-down area of a ceiling or cornice, and can provide a high level of direct light. It is generally placed over a featured sales area or the entrance to a key department. It also can be placed around the perimeter of a store or along one wall to visually expand a space or draw attention to it. Either fluorescent or incandescent lamps can be installed in a soffit with a suitable eggcrate diffuser or louver at the bottom.

Accent Lighting. Accent lighting is used to highlight key titles or special display features within a space. Low-voltage halogen lamps or other types that produce narrow beam spreads are a good choice for such effects. Special effects can also be created by fixtures that break light into many small, bright spots.

Emergency, Exit, and Fire Lights. Emergency, exit, and fire lights are safety devices required by building ordinances. Emergency lighting is supported by battery packs. Self-powered, rechargeable tritium-gas exit signs that glow for up to 12 to 20 years without consuming electrical energy are available. Fire lights, which are visual fire alarm devices recommended in ADA guidelines and activated when a designated fire alarm is pulled, are also available, and frequently required by local ordinances.

Lighting the Store Exterior

Lighting the areas around a bookstore or shopping center can have a substantial influence on the establishment's image and customer traffic volume. Good

ABOVE: Lanterns, back- and spot-lighted signs, and light spilling out of show windows add to the dramatic, exterior night-lighting of this superstore. ABOVE R: 2' x 2', 2 light, U40 fluorescent light fixtures fit neatly into a standard ceiling grid. Typical pull-down incandescent accent lights, pendant lamps, smoke detectors, sprinklers, speaker system, security devices, and air conditioning outlets are also enclosed by this ceiling at LIBERTIES, Boca Raton, Fla.

outdoor lighting design uses a variety of techniques: building floodlighting, area lighting, walkway lighting, landscape lighting, roadway lighting, and sign lighting.

To produce a maintained level of 5 footcandles over a large area, the following approximate watts-per-square-foot will be obtained using these GE Lamps:

Lucalox (R)	.1	Mercury Vapor	.22
Deluxe Lucalox (R)	.12	Incandescent	.54
Multi-Vapor (R)	.16		

Regardless of the lamp chosen, light poles should not be spaced more than four times their height apart from one another. Wider spacing will create glare and/or dark areas between poles. For both motorist and pedestrian safety and comfort, it is important to avoid unnecessary glare.

Application of Lighting Design

Lighting design involves selecting and locating the appropriate lamps and fixtures to satisfy merchandising needs. Our designers develop concepts to determine what the lighting should be, not only to satisfy requirements, but also to complement the

118 PART 1

architectural features and the character of the interior space. After exploring several optional sketches, our designers develop a lighting plan to accomplish those goals. The lighting plan is part of the construction drawings (Chapter 11), and is sometimes referred to as a lighting or reflected ceiling plan. However, each of these plans has distinct characteristics.

Lighting Plan

A lighting plan is prepared for independent bookstore projects to show types and locations of light fixtures and controls. It is often used to communicate the concepts of the lighting design to you and your contractors.

Reflected Ceiling Plan

A reflected ceiling plan is used primarily in bookstore design work for complex ceiling systems that have several changes in elevations, materials, and soffits. In

addition to lighting equipment, it also shows such other ceiling appliance items as HVAC registers, smoke detectors, speakers, video monitors, and sprinklers. A reflected ceiling plan often indicates how lights are switched and where switches are located.

Power and Signal Plan

The power and signal plan is a floor plan that shows electrical wall, fixture, and floor outlets, computer cabling, modems, music and video systems, telephone outlets, and other devices that use power. Service panels, electrical line diagrams, and security and light-control switches can be added.

Power Consumption Constraints

Lighting systems for new and remodeled retail bookstores should be designed to meet all needs yet not exceed 6 watts per square foot. These constraints have a strong influence on the design of interior lighting of all book and general retail stores.

ABOVE L: Perimeter case work lighting illuminates the floor, merchandise and perimeter ceiling. This photo also illustrates ceiling-mounted exit signs, a new type of air condition outlet and pictogram graphics in the Parenting section. UBS Kids, Madison, Wis. ABOVE: 3 tube, 24 cell, 2' x 4' deep cell parabolic fluorescent luminaires, mounted in an open ceiling grid, help create a dramatic retail environment. Humboldt State University Bookstore, Arcata, Calif.

CHAPTER 9
SIGNAGE AND GRAPHICS DESIGN

There are eight basic kinds of store signing: storefront, directional, directory, category, subcategory, policy, promotional, and control. Each type of sign has its own distinct purpose.

Graphics Design

Graphics design is not purely an art, nor is it a science; rather, it involves aspects of both. Good graphics design is an effective blending of creative intuition, logical analysis, and technical know-how. This approach can provide distinctive signing and graphics programs that communicate efficiently and extend the point-of-sale marketing opportunities of the bookstore.

Small-Bookstore Graphics Systems

For identification and merchandising requirements, a small bookstore may need only a storefront sign, a modest number of category signs, and a sign each indicating store hours, check cashing policy, return policy, and a listing of services. Exit signs and other governmental regulation signs may also be needed. We will cover those requirements in greater detail later in this chapter.

Large-Bookstore Graphics Systems

The graphics system for a large bookstore follows the same track as that for a small store, only on a larger scale. The internal arrangement of a large store may be very complex, with security or restricted areas requiring a complete system of interior directional signs. A large store may also have several floors, requiring a system of floor directories at stairs, escalators, and elevator lobbies. Multi-level stores usually require a graphics system with a high degree of flexibility to accommodate the many department title, category, policy, and service message signs, all of which are subject to frequent changes.

Banners and flags are nice graphic touches that can be used in large spaces to make them more pleasant people-places in which to browse and buy books. We have worked on large bookstore projects on military bases, in national parks, in medical centers, and on college campuses with long distances between areas or

Striking white lettering announces the name of the store. Simple awning treatments are favored by booksellers to draw attention to their shops in a tasteful manner. Bay Books, Coronado, Calif.

Brick, stone, and fabric awnings, combined with gold leaf and white detailing on the glass show windows, create an interesting effect on the front of this Greenwich Village bookstore. Cooper Square Bookstore, New York City.

Promotional copy for table top signage should be bright and to the point. Bluewater Books & Charts, Fort Lauderdale, Fla.

buildings and complicated site locations. These situations require various systems of *exterior* signs, which may include map-type directories to help orient customers, many of whom are visiting for the first time.

Superstore Graphics Systems

The sometimes overwhelming size of some large, multi-level superstores and college stores, with their mixture of sales, activity, and community-room areas, creates a need for even larger, well coordinated sign systems. These stores require a system that communicates equally well with customers and staff, whether they are browsing, working, walking slowly, or moving more rapidly through the store.

Basic sign requirements of superstores are the same as those for large college stores. In both types of stores, there is a fundamental need for highly individual department and section directories and shelf labels. These graphic features help customers find the books they want, and also help stocking clerks find the proper location for incoming books.

Shopping Center Graphics Requirements

Shopping centers exert controls on the quality of tenant signing by including sign design criteria statements in lease agreements. These criteria may impose limitations on the size and shape of signs. Quality materials and craftsmanship are always insisted upon. The larger centers establish a design review committee empowered to accept or reject a design on aesthetic grounds. An example of typical regional mall sign criteria can be found in Appendix I.

Sign Code Information and Permits

Municipal sign permits that grant permission to install exterior signs are required for all retail stores. These permits are generally obtained by the sign contractor. To ensure that all exterior and interior signs of an existing building will satisfy code requirements, either you or your sign contractor should check with your local department of building and safety and/or your local fire department.

Regional and Departmental Signs

Regional and departmental signs are of several types. Most are fabricated with adhesive-backed lettering composed and applied to plexiglas, wood, medium-density fiberboard (MDF), or Masonite backgrounds. More elaborate regional signs can be hand-painted or silk-screened onto standard background materials.

Category Signs

The most important graphics found in a bookstore are category signs. These signs "tell and sell": they tell what you have to sell, and help customers find it. Category signs are most often made with vinyl-film letters applied to precut and painted strips of cardboard or styrene (thin, opaque, lightweight plastic sheeting made for graphic work). Letraset (rub-off) transfer letters (available from large art stores) are also used to create category-sign copy. Large stores use sign machines to produce quality category signs on short notice.

Lighted Graphics

Back-lighted, edge-lighted, face-lighted, and spotlighted bookstore signs and graphic panels are popular ways to create strong departmental images. Back-light graphics are made in many configurations with neon outline letters on silk-screened panels, individual face-lighted letters, or individual back-lighted letters.

Individual neon-lighted letters mounted to a channel and applied to the face of the building were prescribed by the sign criteria of this new strip center mall. Webster's Books, Ann Arbor, Mich.

Neon Signs and Graphics

Neon is the term generally used to describe lighted tubing of all colors. Neon is an inert, colorless, gaseous element. When contained in a glass vacuum tube through which an electrical current is passed, a reddish-orange glow is produced. Lighted neon signs are easy to maintain and, under normal conditions, have a very long life.

Neon-lighted signs are visible under all day and nighttime conditions, which is a district advantage. Neon design elements can be combined with other techniques to create interesting graphics. Neon is also used to enliven existing signs and graphics. White-, green-, dark-, light-, and ice-blue, dark and light green, jasmine yellow, apricot, rose, amber, flame, magenta, red and ruby-red colors are available in neon light.

Black-Light Signs

Ultraviolet illumination of fluorescent materials, known as *black light*, can be styled and designed to create a very dramatic effect. While successful black-light signage needs closely controlled conditions, in most bookstore environments, it is possible to achieve great black-light signage for mystery, magic, horror, and comic book design.

Lighted neon signage color should relate to colors in the department or space where the sign will be installed. University Bookstore, Madison, Wis.

ABOVE: Individual neon-lighted letters. Sides are made of metal with an acrylic face and mounted to the facade of the building. Moody Bookstore, Chicago, Ill. *LEFT: Thick exterior signs cast shadows, increasing their legibility.* Webster's Books, Ann Arbor, Mich.

Lighted, multi-colored exterior sign is a shaped graphic with incise carved letters and painted art. Chapters Bookstore & Cafe', Shelburne, Vt.

ABOVE L: Gondola sub-directories list categories contained in adjoining fixtures. The purpose is to help the customer find the category and the store clerk find the location to re-stock titles they are working with. Webster's Books, Ann Arbor, Mich. *BELOW L: Endcap gondola sub-directories can also state fixture numbers, directional arrows and store name, concentrated in a small space.* Humboldt State University Bookstore, Arcata, Calif.

Electromechanical Signs

Electromechanical signage, generally used for news bulletin boards, can be a very effective way to announce new titles, special events, promotions, discounts, and bargains in high-traffic areas. Messages can be easily changed and repeated over and over again. These signs can be especially effective in business bookstores when they repeat stock quotations and general news. Because of their ability to instantly add or change a merchandising message from a central control point, electromechanical signage in promotional bookstores can be a big asset.

Control Signs

Control signs are notices required by building codes and for ADA compliance. *Men, Women, Authorized Personnel, Manager*, and *Exit* are typical signs often required by building codes. The copy for these graphics may be applied directly to doors, windows, or walls. Engraved laminate plaques are also used for this purpose and are attached to doors and wall surfaces with security mountings or industrial double-faced tape.

Typical category signs are used for wall cases, gondolas and other freestanding store fixtures. DeAnza College Bookstore, Cupertino, Calif.

We design store directories in a variety of shapes, to be freestanding, fitted around columns or mounted to a wall. LEFT: Freestanding directory with "Where to find the books you want" header, category listings and floor plans. Webster's Books, Ann Arbor, Mich. *RIGHT: Directory surrounds a column and includes a changeable-letter Coming Events board and space for special messages.* University Bookstore, Madison, Wis.

Audio Signage Support

Video sign messages can become so complex that it may be necessary to reinforce the video part of the sign with an audio backup message to make sure that people understand them. Audio signage support systems are popular in children's departments and in music and specialty bookstores.

Changeable Signs and Letter Boards

Nearly every large bookstore needs to display current events, the time, date, and other data. Such a display can easily be accomplished with changeable letters or copy strips. Some directories are designed to utilize computer-generated copy strips that are produced in the store. The typefaces and composition of the changeable letter strips should match or be compatible with other store signing.

Video Message Signage

In areas that require a constant message turnover, you should consider using ROM-CDs, VCRs, and other computer-controlled video output devices. One can store many thousands of messages in the central computer, and these can be displayed at various remote locations throughout the bookstore, using a simple television monitor.

Individual moulded lettering with metallic finish was used for the interior storefront. RIT Bookstore, Rochester, N.Y.

Standard or custom-designed banners can add a sense of place, balance, color and excitement to large-volume atriums, foyers and entrances. Flags may also be used to create period and geographic themes. University of Cincinnati Bookstore, Cincinnati, Ohio. For more ideas, please refer to the Earthling Bookstore, Chapter 6.

Banners and Flags

Large, multi-level stores sometimes have sufficient space to effectively use banners and flags. They add color and movement, and can announce important sales events. There are many types of banners: long banners with lovely designs that seem to float, slowly and gracefully, streamers that ripple or shimmer, and metal banners that hang vertically, adding color and reflections.

Flags are usually rectangular shapes, flown horizontally, whereas banners come in a variety of horizontal and vertical shapes. Medieval (King Arthur) theme flags can be adventuresome in children's departments. Flags of countries displayed in a row make exciting decorations in travel departments.

ADA: Meeting the Needs of Aging and Physically Disabled People

In this era of aging and disabled populations, bookstore facilities are used more and more by elderly and physically disabled people. Moreover, many local building ordinances require retail stores to comply with provisions of the Americans With Disabilities Act (ADA).

The new law makes no mention of removing any existing or otherwise necessary signage that is useful to the non-handicapped. An overview of key points in ADA regulations that can affect your store is included in the *ADA Accessibility Guidelines (ADAAG)*. Printed in Table 9.1 are some of *ADAAG*'s major references to signage; there are, however, many other references to signage made throughout the guidelines.

LEFT: Handicapped check-out stations must be provided and identified with appropriate signage. Public rest rooms must be identified with the accessibility and male/female symbols. Right: Approved international symbol of accessibility. The pictogram's border dimension must be 6". Raised and brailled pictograms are required at the entrance to bookstores. Moody Bookstore, Chicago, Ill. For rest room symbols, please see UBS Kids, Chapter 6.

Table 9.1   Excerpts from the *ADAAG* Signage Guidelines

All signs that shall comply with ADA requirements and spaces of accessible facilities which shall be identified by the International Symbol of Accessibility are:

(A) Parking spaces designated as reserved for physically handicapped people; (B) passenger loading zones; (C) accessible entrances; (D) accessible toilet and facilities.

Technical Requirements

Signage required to be accessible shall comply with the following:

Character Proportion - Letters and numbers on signs required shall have a width-to-height ratio between 3:5 and 1:1 and a stroke width-to-height ratio between 1:5 and 1:10.

Color Contrast - Characters and symbols shall contrast with their background - either light characters on a dark background or dark characters on a light background.

Raised or Indented Characters or Symbols - Letters and numbers on signs shall be raised or incised and shall be sans serif characters. Symbols or pictographs on signs shall be raised or indented.

Symbols of Accessibility - Accessible facilities required to be identified, shall display the international symbol of accessibility.

Mounting Location and Height - Interior ADA signage shall be located alongside the door on the latch side and shall be mounted at a height of between 54 in and 66 in (1370 mm and 1675 mm) above the finished door. Mounting for such signage shall be so that a person may approach within 3" (76 mm) of signage without encountering protruding objects or standing within the swing of a door.

SIGNAGE AND GRAPHICS DESIGN   **129**

Control signs are required for exits, fire extinguishers, fire alarm instructions, notices of authorized entry, exits and handicapped accessibility. The better the graphics are organized, the more effective the visual communication. Millersville State University Bookstore, Millersville, Penn.

LEFT: Gold leaf logo applied to a black vinyl background is used as a focal point over store entrance. Moody Bookstore, Chicago, Ill.
RIGHT: Large-scale exterior logo applied to face of bookstore building. Yaesu book center, Tokyo, Japan.

Specialty Signage: Decals and Flexible Magnets

Decals, which are used for a variety of purposes , are often attached to show windows or displayed near the front of the store. Decals provide information about credit cards, fire control, alarms, and security. They can be in the form of pictograms indicating accessibility information or *No Food, No Pets, No Smoking, No Backpacks.*

Magnetic strip signs are used along the edges of metal shelves to provide subcategory information. Magnetic signs are printed on flexible sheets of vinyl paper laminated to steel foil and cast into thin strips. The magnetized foil acts as a magnet, and with sufficient attraction on metal shelf edges, holds the strip securely in place. Magnetic signs are useful to designate stock areas with messages such as *Alpha by Author* and *Alphabetically by Subject.*

Sign Code Information and Permits

Municipal sign permits that grant permission to install exterior signs are required for all retail stores. These permits are generally obtained by the sign contractor. To ensure that all exterior and interior signs of an existing building will satisfy code requirements, either you or your sign contractor should check with your local department of building and safety and/or your local fire department.

Bookmarks, Stationery, Wrappings, and Shopping Bags

Translating your store's graphics designs into logos, bookmarks, stationery, wrappings, and store bags is an important activity. Care and taste must be exercised in the choice of typefaces, paper, printing, wrapping paper, store bags, and stationery. Many large stores use four sizes of bags with colors and designs that add advertising and visibility to the aesthetic quality of their business image.

Future Changes

All bookstores have continuous merchandising changes that result in the need to periodically change and update their signing needs. Revisions can be handled either by a firm that provides you with ongoing consulting design services, or by the use of signing manuals that we can develop for you. Development of a graphics manual requires a great deal of coordination with you, but such coordination is necessary if you are considering entirely new kinds of signs or uses. Properly designed signing manuals may be the best method of identifying and reordering sign components.

Graphics are really a lot of fun to work with. It is the one area where a lot of tone and color can be added at a modest cost.

Regional sign is used for departmental identification. Graphic was back-painted on a clear acrylic panel and hung with aircraft cable. Deitrick-VPI Bookstore, Blacksburg, Va.

CHAPTER 10

ELECTRONICS IN THE BOOKSTORE

There are three major groups of electronic equipment used by independent booksellers to aid customers and help employees sell more books: communications, music and video, and POS systems.

Communications

A telephone is the primary electronics requirement for a bookstore. Sounds simple enough, but let us consider that this sentence describes a telephone for voice communication in and out of the store. Today we are really dealing with an internal communications system linking the cashiers, the back room, offices, and work station staffs. In larger stores communications extend to distribution centers and warehouses. In very large organizations, multi-store communications are complex.

Today telephone communication lines with modems are essential. They are required for communicating electronic orders and confirmations linking the store, publishers, distributors, and book wholesalers. The linking of POS (point of sale), terminals (cash registers), with a main frame PC (personal computer), and collecting of in-store sales data and management information, is often done through telephone lines.

Many stores need a fax (facsimile) machine to send orders directly to publishers, distributors and wholesalers, and for inter-store communication and communication with key customers. Telephone lines are used for credit card approval, communication with banks, and other credit sources.

Telephone lines are an important component of security systems. They are used to link the store to security firms and often police and fire departments. It is easy to see how a relatively small store can find itself with twelve or more telephone lines.

In-Store Music and Video Systems

Many independent booksellers feature music in their stores in one form or another. Music adds to the ambiance and appeal of the store. Music systems in most small shops are simply a radio or tape recorder. There is a better way. Stores may contract at a very reasonable price with one of several national suppliers of music via satellite. A small dish antenna is mounted on the roof of the building and wired to

Great literature, N.Y. Times bestsellers at 40 percent off, and a customer information and service desk with ROM-CD and computer capability have redefined the image of this successful, upscale branch mall bookstore. University Bookstore, Hilldale Mall, Madison, Wis.

an internal speaker system. Sound complicated? Technically yes, but from a practical point of view, these systems are reasonably priced, easily installed and maintained by the provider.

Video systems are provided for information, education, entertainment, marketing, and overall store ambiance. Video monitors mounted on the ceiling are protected, easy to see, and attract customers' attention. Monitors should be placed where they can be seen and controlled from a service desk. The convenience of being able to change the tape, rewind, replay, change the volume, and otherwise control the video monitors, is an important consideration. Equipment for mounting video monitors to the ceiling is readily available and reasonably priced. Each monitor requires a separate VCR for personalized programming. There is a trend toward using monitors for individual and group book promotions. These promotional video tapes, trailers, etc. are provided by leading publishers. The ability to change the videotapes from the work station is important.

Discreet security cameras, recording onto 72-hour VCR tapes, can give booksellers a state-of-the-art method for combating in-store theft.

ABOVE: Cashier station with POS terminal, cash drawer, scanner, and printer. Moody Bookstore, Chicago, Ill. *RIGHT: Cashier counter with raised ledge to conceal unattractive wiring at back of CRTs.* Webster's Books, Lansing, Mich. *BELOW: CRT information station with storage cabinet, CRT, and pull-out keyboard feature.* University Bookstore, Hilldale Mall, Madison, Wis.

POS Systems

There are POS systems on the market that are reliable and provide good information. In fact, most POS systems can provide far more data than most stores use. We estimate that less than 10% of the bookstores in the United States use the systems they have bought to the extent possible. Most stores seem to use POS systems for electronic ordering, cashier functions, receipts, and input of inventory. Daily sales reports are generated and provide these same stores with the ability to look up and determine whether a particular title is in stock. Beyond that, the majority of the systems' capabilities remain untouched. The system updates are common; their implementation, however, is not. The ABA will be happy to furnish a list of systems used by most booksellers. Major distributors, Baker & Taylor, and wholesalers offer sophisticated packaged system programs that are reliable and effective. Because of the rapid changes taking place, it is best that the prospective bookseller contact these organizations directly to receive the most up-to-date information on their offerings.

POS System Hardware

There is continuous development in POS hardware. High resolution CRT's (cathode ray tubes), cash drawers, and printers of all types get better, smaller, and

less expensive every year. Providing a home for all this hardware, wiring, and connections to and from components has added substantially to the cost of electrical work required to build an up-to-date bookstore facility.

Electronic Merchandising Tools

A secret to the success of independent bookstores in the 90s and beyond, involves building in the support tools that salespeople need to succeed.

The right tools make it easier to hire people. You simply look for people capable of using the tools - generally nice people with sincere smiles, people who like to work with others and enjoy making people comfortable. With CD-ROM computers available to look up information, on-line title base information, electronic special order systems in place, the mystery of working in independent bookstores can be minimized. Time spent in training can get closer to the point of dealing with the retail matters.

Electronic merchandising tools simplify the store's ability to adjust its title mix and add to categories where appropriate. It takes more than rationality to sell books and sidelines in this increasingly complex, saturated book market. Emotional appeals and visual communications, backed up by outstanding POS systems, are key to a specialty bookseller's success - continually employing concepts that appeal to the sensibilities and technology of a specific market will help make you a successful bookseller.

ABOVE L: Tape deck, CD player, amplifier, and VCRs, each mounted on individual pull-out shelves installed adjacent to customer service desk. ABOVE R: Two video monitors mounted on the ceiling are controlled by VCRs described above. BELOW: Customer service ROM-CD station includes CRT, keyboard, printer, PC, and modem. UBS Kids, Madison, Wisc.

The Future

Given its rate of growth in the past decade, it is hard to imagine that we will not see a greater explosion in electronic gadgetry and equipment wizardry by the turn of the century.

Where does that leave us? Not entirely up in the air. We can deal with the equipment program and electronic systems now available to us. Small bookstores can successfully run their businesses just as efficiently as a super chain store. The good part about it is that many of these POS systems are modular. They can be installed all at once or over a period of time. POS, electronic ordering, and inventory control systems are better today than they have ever been in the history of the book business.

CHAPTER 11
PUTTING IT ALL TOGETHER

Naming the Store

Design themes and names for bookstores are logically arrived at after a careful study of the market and location (The Corner Bookstore, Bay Books, or The Fisherman's Bookshop). A name or theme may identify the number of titles or book category (The 50,000 Bookshop, the Professional Bookstore, The Museum Judaica, or Ballet Bookshop). The preference of the owner or a bookselling specialty may be the theme (The Tree of Life Bookshop, The Mystery Bookshop, The Dickens, or Literary Bookshop). In many cases, the name often reflects the design theme (The Gothic Bookstore).

The most obvious name to give a bookstore is that of the owner, (C. Johnson Bookseller or Brian Prince Bookseller). Occasionally, a seal or crest of an institutional owner is made up and used as a trademark, and then becomes the basis of the interior design.

Names often used for bookstores are those of fictional or historical characters or settings (Webster's Books, The Sam Houston or The Canterbury Bookshop). These shops may be authentic reproductions based on accurate research of the period.

Names can underscore geographic themes (Sail Away Travel Bookshop, Europa, or Gulliver's Books and Maps). Other bookstore names come from the type of merchandise sold in the store (Literary and Publishing World, the Art and Type Bookstore, or the Paperback Bookshop). Almost any area of interest can be developed into a design theme or focal point (The Christian Bookshop, The Design Center Bookshop, or The Computer Bookstore).

Sometimes bookstores never get named. Most often this happens in airline terminals, department stores, and the like. In such cases, the bookstore is designed as a part of the building in which it is located and is simply planned as the nonentity it is destined to become. Don't let that happen to your bookstore, particularly if it is a "Lilliputian Place," a children's bookstore or department.

Final Review

When all the conceptual design elements - store fixtures, floors, walls, ceilings, lighting, colors, and graphics - have been finalized and coordinated with the plans,

Dark wood display fixtures, green glass shades, comfortable leather-upholstered chairs, live plants and neutral background colors are consistent design themes used throughout the store. Visual merchandise props are used to focus attention on sale tables. Chapters Bookstore & Cafe', Jelly Mill Shopping Center, Shelburne, Vt.

the project schedule and cost estimates should be checked against the building program. The best way to do this is to schedule a final review and coordination meeting that brings together the project architect, mechanical consulting engineers, and others who have worked with the plans. The meeting should resolve any open questions. This is the time to review the budget, building permits, scheduling, and to make sure your store design and plans meet requirements for the elderly and handicapped. It is also the time to review sketches, colors, finishes, details, and materials, and to make final adjustments.

Project Plans

When minor structural or mechanical changes are for one-floor projects, the building plan and design information is usually shown on a single drawing. For multi-floor projects, two or more drawings and specifications are required. In larger and more complicated projects, separate sets of architectural, structural, and mechanical drawings and indexed specifications are mandatory. As many as fifty of these contract documents may be required to cover in detail the work expected and materials required to build a large store or remodel an existing one.

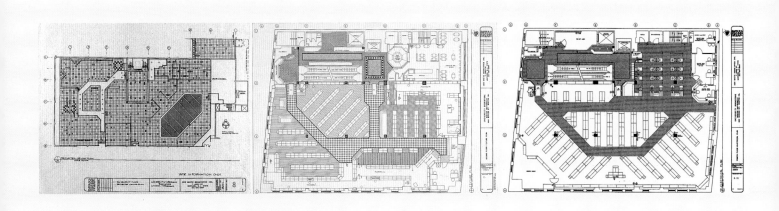

ABOVE L: Reflected ceiling plan. UNL Nightingale Bookshop, Lincoln, Neb. *CENTER: Coordinated second-floor finish and general book department store fixture plan. RIGHT: Coordinated fourth-floor finish and textbook department store fixture plan.* Charlesbank Bookshops & Cafe', Boston, Mass.

Store Fixture Plans

The store fixture plan, elevations, and fixture details of a small one-floor bookstore can be shown on a single large drawing. For larger and multi-level bookstores, the layout must be shown floor-by-floor in a larger set of plans. In the case of very complicated, large stores, it is a good idea to have a key overall plan of the store drawn at 1/8-inch-to-the-foot scale, and also larger (1/4-inch) scale plans of individual departments made and keyed to the smaller plan. Very large drawings are unwieldy and difficult for everyone to handle.

Separate plans are usually made for (1) the store fixtures, (2) graphics, (3) sales floor furniture (including stools, ladders, browsing tables, and chairs), (4) office furniture, (5) color schemes, (6) floor coverings, (7) communications (telephones, CRTs, and computers), and (8) lighting, unless, of course, one or more of these items is included in the general set of building construction plans. Each store fixture, piece of furniture, and graphic item should be coded and numbered on the plans. These documents are then supplemented by written specifications and used for pricing, coordination, installation, merchandising, and reference purposes. Specifications are clearly written, technical descriptions of the work to be performed. Specifications should fully describe the material to be used and services to be rendered.

Sources of Store Fixtures

There are four primary sources of bookstore fixtures. Your first two options are to build simple fixtures on site, either with or without the help of a local contractor.

Your third choice is to buy used bookstore fixtures. Used fixtures, generally sold by popular makers of standard fixtures, are fairly often advertised, usually by brand name, in the *ABA Newswire* and the *Publishers Weekly.*

Finally, you may choose to buy new bookstore fixtures. Four or more manufacturers display standard, new store fixtures at the annual ABA Convention. There is a wide variety of quality and value displayed among them. They are all adequate for short-term (1-, 2- or 3-year) lease deals.

Store Fixture Manufacturers

There are many quality independent store fixture manufacturers, also known as fixture contractors, who are equipped to fabricate, deliver, and install complete bookstore fixtures. Many of the large firms are members of the National Association of Store Fixture Manufacturers, who will gladly furnish you with a list of their members.

Because installing and setting up a bookstore is such a specialized and demanding undertaking, it is best to work with store fixture manufacturers who have experience with bookstores.

The Fixture Contractor Bid List

The fixture contractor invited to bid or negotiate a contract to fabricate your new equipment should be financially sound. Over the years, some fixture contractors have unfortunately gone out of business during the course of a project, leaving clients high and dry.

Our many years of experience dealing with contractors throughout the U.S. can be an invaluable asset to you in determining which bidders, in addition to your own, to choose from.

The Fixture Contractor's Bid

Final plans and complete specifications with bid forms are supplied to each fixture contractor invited to quote on the project. The reason for this process is to assure that competitive bids submitted by various contractors are based on identical requirements.

Five to ten days are required to solicit and receive store fixture bids for most bookstore projects. All quotations should be furnished on the bid forms that we provide. There is a provision to accommodate exceptions or alternatives that the contractor may submit. We will assist you in analyzing the bids you receive.

Awarding the Store Fixture Contract

All small and most large bookstore fixture contracts are awarded to a single supplier. The potential of a larger contract creates a better bidding-price atmosphere, and usually results in better overall price and coordination. There are, of course, occasions when the size of the project and the date when the store fixtures are needed make it practical and necessary to split the contract and purchase the store fixture equipment from several store fixture manufacturers.

Successful fixture contractors should be notified of their selection by the store planner and confirmed by a letter of intent from us. A contract or purchase order in the agreed amount is prepared, executed, and sent to the successful bidder.

Approval of Shop Drawings and Material Samples

When the contract has been awarded, we supply the chosen store fixture contractor with samples of color and finish choices, and with other relevant information required to prepare shop drawings and complete the project. In turn, the fixture contractor provides us with duplicate sets of several important documents for review and approval. These include the proposed schedule (timed to coincide with the activities of the builder/developer of the project), and a complete set of shop drawings. Shop drawings are made to illustrate the store fixture contractor's interpretation of the intent of the contract drawings.

When these documents and samples are approved, the fixture production begins. The builder is given the final color schedules for painting the interior and, if necessary, the exterior of the store.

Project Management: Follow-Up, Expediting, and Coordinating

While the fixture manufacturer is primarily responsible for maintaining the quality and scheduling of the store fixtures, we follow each step. For small- and medium-sized projects, a trip to the site from time to time may be sufficient. For larger projects, in response to specific requests, we often arrange for a part- or full-

The construction process. ABOVE L: Following demolition and clearing out the space, partitions are laid out and erected. CENTER: Partitions and ceilings are covered. RIGHT: Paint finishes, fixtures, lighting and graphics are added to create the final retail environment. Charlesbank Bookshops & Cafe', Boston, Mass.

time project manager to provide for coordination, and to make on-site observations of the bookstore fixtures and fabricated items, such as the graphics. For large projects, we both must meet with the architect and builder regularly throughout the construction period.

Change Orders

Many bookstores built in new as well as older buildings require some changes in construction and store fixture contracts during the progress of the work. Careful planning and complete, professionally prepared drawings and specifications can keep these changes to a minimum. But because bookselling is still more of an art than a science, new merchandising ideas are added and dropped, and new departments or services have a way of creeping into plans for lighting, store fixtures, and graphics. These changes can be fairly easily accommodated. But structural changes are much more involved and, therefore, more costly.

Approval of Payments

During and at the end of the project, we review the invoices submitted by contractors. We review and certify all payments to be made by you to the store fixture manufacturers for completed work. It is the consultant's responsibility to see that the plans and specifications are followed and that the bookstore interior is built as designed. For large projects, it is usually the architect's responsibility to approve the builder's requisitions for payment and to see that the general contractor complies with your building plans and specifications.

Completing the Project

About five weeks before the scheduled completion of the job, it is a good idea to get a solid fix on the status of every element of the project: the building, interior and exterior signs, carpet, computers, security systems, etc. This is the time to break bottlenecks and verify that fabrication and construction is on schedule. Once the schedule is confirmed, an opening date should be set and opening media advertising, publicity, and promotional activities arranged. Books must be ordered, and personnel and merchandise move-in also must be scheduled. It is extremely difficult to change previously set dates. Check all these details early.

Everybody Pitches In

All of us - our staffs, the architect, the builder, and the fixture, graphics, and other contractors - should, in the final days of completion, assist in the expediting, scheduling, and supervision of every activity necessary to open the bookstore. These can include taking down construction signs and barricades, washing windows, cleaning lighting fixture lenses, removing trash, and, within contract limits, generally policing the exterior and interior of the bookstore. Completion of the construction project signals the need to schedule building, electrical, mechanical, and fire inspections of the premises, and to obtain the Certificate of Occupancy where it is required.

To prevent last-minute rushes, the bookstore staff will often receive, process, mark, move, and stock fixtures while interior construction is still underway.

Then, one day, everything falls into place, and with a sigh of relief you realize that your bookstore is ready for its simple opening, or its lavish grand opening.

Now, your bookstore is ready to do what is was planned to do: sell books! Good luck!

PART TWO

ANTHOLOGY

Part Two presents an anthology of plans, photographs, and design sketches of small, medium, large, and super bookstores.

In this anthology you will find yourself on a visual journey through plans and illustrations of 24 wonderful bookstores: a cross-section of unique bookstores as they appeared when they were built.

The bookstores were selected from more than 600 to appeal to a wide audience of booksellers and professional store planners. The bookstores illustrated are not only distinguished for their contribution to the bookselling profession, but are also representative of their type of planning, merchandising, and interior architecture. If you should ever visit any of these stores, you will quickly discover that they have come a long way from where they began.

When looking at photographs of early bookstores, the important point to keep in mind is not its age, but how vital its appeal is. To keep the appearance of a retail store alive is to keep alive the store itself. In that sense, all the bookstores shown here are vital and alive; they applaud the people who own and operate them now, and applaud other bookstores like them that have made their own equally important contribution to the bookselling profession. In a few years from now, there will again be far too many imaginative bookstores to contain in a single anthology.

LIBERTIES
Fine Books & Music
Boca Raton, Fla.

An Independent Super Bookstore

Vald and Sheri Svekis set out to build a stunning, unique, world-class superstore with classical details, beautiful music and lovely graphics, where books and more books are the thing.

LIBERTIES caters particularly to customers who like individual attention. The owners and staff take great pride in the special-order service that supplements the wider general stock. There is an experienced and friendly staff here to help the children to choose from their wide selection of books and cassettes. The stock ranges from cloth books through teenage fiction and non-fiction. They also stock educational books. Browsers of all ages are most welcome.

LIBERTIES was designed as a store that would be fresh and different. A store that people would come to love in the first 30 seconds. We were not interested in creating "a good looking store, but what a great department" reactions. We were interested in combining the ideas that together create the "Boca" environment and attitude - high ceilings, wood floors, beautifully detailed fixtures, articulated mouldings, receding color, elegant graphics, quiet light.

From the beginning we believed the store would be a success and it would be huge. It is.

ABOVE: The Mediterranean-style architecture of Mizner Park shopping center. RIGHT: Neutral interior tones focus customers' attention on book presentations and promotions.

The classical design theme of the LIBERTIES interior is based on the Tuscan Latin order, the simplest and most solid of all formal architectural orders. This order conveys ideas of strength and simplicity. It agreeably complements the architecture of Mizner Park and helps create an easy bookselling environment. We used Tuscan proportions, forms and components for the lighting and graphic cornices and details that make up a considerable part of the store's classical texture, ambiance and relevance to Boca Raton. Five store-fixture manufacturers were employed to make, deliver and install the architectural woodwork and equipment. 110,000 titles are stocked in this memorable 12,500-square-foot independent super bookstore.

WIT & WISDOM BOOKSELLERS
Lawrenceville, N.J.

A General Independent Bookstore

BELOW: WIT & WISDOM BOOKSELLERS is a browser's delight, stocking mostly current fiction and literature, with a good selection of cloth titles in all categories.

A rich retail ambiance is created with low-surface-brightness lighting fixtures and a monochromatic color scheme that uses three values of gray. Mahogany fixtures and rolling ladders complete the look. The store has a good selection of children's books, greeting cards, magazines and study guides.

The knowledgeable staff provides mail-order, special-order, and personal service on request.

FLICKERTAIL BOOKSHOP
University of North Dakota, Grand Forks, N.D.

A Victorian-Style General Bookshop

RIGHT: Meticulously researched and executed, this bookshop was designed and built by local craftsmen to reflect the vernacular architecture of the region's Victorian period.

Custom white store fixtures with fretwork details are placed on black oak and red carpet floor covering. Stained glass was reproduced by local artists. Authentic brass reproductions of chandeliers hang from a painted, beaded wood ceiling.

The shop was largely destroyed in a fire of mysterious origins in 1990.

BOOK SHOP & SALES
Independence Hall, Philadelphia, Pa.

Historic Site - Specialty Bookshop

This small bookshop fitting neatly into the east wing of Independence Hall caters particularly to customers wishing to extend the experience of their visit to this great national shrine. The staff takes great pride in the special services that supplement the wider general stock of books, posters, prints, maps, postcards and museum quality productions.

The design of the store was inspired by the overall feeling of applied mouldings and painted wood surfaces - few shops in Philadelphia were furnished with natural wood fixtures during the colonial period. We think the design reflects just enough history to help in the retail effort but not enough to get in the way. The design is a symbolic rather than a faithful reproduction of a shop of the time.

C. JOHNSON BOOKSELLER
London, Ontario, Canada
An Independent General Bookstore

This is a bookstore for book lovers. The store has a crisp, contemporary, rich, refined shop design. It is all gray-relieved with white walls, deep green carpet and countertops, and hushed in tone. The store's appeal is to the successful individual who wants the best Canadian, American and British publications.

The store fixtures reach from the floor to the ceiling and are banded by a red oak rolling ladder track. The store offers a dramatic view from its open show windows at night. This puts more merchandise on view and allows for use of imaginative publishers' display materials. This is a shop on the go for a customer base that is on the move - upward and onward. This is a store that prides itself on service. Chris and Tim and the Johnson family are friendly and knowledgeable. The store is well-arranged and the selection and service are good. It has a knack for keeping popular, hard-to-find books in stock.

COMMUNITY BOOKSTORE
Brooklyn, N.Y.

A General Independent Bookstore

This is a well-established, 980-square-foot, fiercely independent bookstore in the Park Slope district of Brooklyn. COMMUNITY BOOKSTORE has succeeded because of its excellent title base and loyal clientele, who have a thing about wanting their own bookstore. Very much a neighborhood shop, with many of its titles classified as literature, the books are arranged alphabetically by author. To further extend its appeal and its market, COMMUNITY BOOKSTORE was renovated and repositioned with an upscale image featuring a new POS inventory control system.

The reimaged interior includes a custom-pattern red carpet, antique metal ceiling, new black store fixtures, black and gold graphics, and tasteful accessories and lighting. As a result, the store is brighter and has found more stock capacity in the same space. The new store is well-accepted and popular with its clientele.

HARRY W. SCHWARTZ BOOKSELLERS
Milwaukee, Wis.

Branch of an Independent General Bookseller

Alvin Dominitz promised us that we would enjoy this shop. And we did. A short time later it was expanded. Located in an affluent part of the city, it is hard not to like this warm, traditional shop. A strip mall bookstore branch of a quality independent bookseller, it has a great selection, knowledgeable staff and lots of charm. It was designed "in house."

This store is attractively and intelligently arranged and provides a soothing color palette. There are a few wicker reading chairs and upholstered love seats. Classical background music is played. Customers shop at this store not only for its selection and values, but because they enjoy the atmosphere. The store is divided into shops within a shop and has one of the most successful bookstore environments found anywhere in the U.S.

It has a good selection of current, hardbound covers and literary gifts, a large collection of coffee-table books on art, architecture, travel, fashion and photography, and an impressive bargain book department. Visual merchandising has become an integral part of the store design.

ABOVE L: The interior volume is used to its greatest potential. A high-ceiling section providing an alternative for overstock is accessed by a roll-around library ladder. BELOW L: View from bargain-book section to front of store. OPPOSITE PAGE: A casual but tailored look is achieved with incandescent track lighting, wicker furniture and wood case work.

POWELL'S BOOKS AT PDX
Portland, Ore.

Specialty Airport Branch Bookshop

This is an inviting bookshop located in the departure concourse of the Portland International Airport - PDX.

Three walls of the store surrounding a center island are stocked from floor to ceiling with a well-organized inventory of new, used, and frontlist bestsellers.

This recently expanded shop, designed by in-house staff, is a place to pick up a book for your next trip out and then sell it back on your return. Travel, mystery, and children's sections offer a fun mix of classic and modern books. The store also has a good selection of local and travel books.

The knowledgeable staff is eager to help. When asked to recommend titles they enthusiastically describe their favorites, and if you are buying a book as a gift, the staff will wrap it for free. Neat!

ABOVE L: Bestsellers, games sections and bargain-book sale table. Below L: Unique arrangement of new and used frontlist science fiction and mystery titles. ABOVE R: High regional, travel and map sections surround low-lighted sale tables. BELOW R: The open-window back of the wood-panel-faced storefront makes the the shop's interior easily visible fron the airport concourse.

Tattered Cover Book Store
Denver, Colo.

A Large Independent Superstore

Described by many as America's favorite bookstore, this multi-level shop is a mix of the old and the new, formal and casual, serious and whimsical, chic and ordinary.

Four heavily stocked floors are bursting with books lined on shelves, piled on tables and stacked on the floor. The store's appeal lies in its wide open spaces. Aisles allow easy movement and there's plenty of room to relax, sit, stand and look; there's also space for lectures, author readings and signings, and other events. The store has an extraordinary, almost overwhelming, inventory and a staff dedicated to making this not only a real fun place but a serious bookstore.

The interior of the store is almost entirely fixtured with wall cases. Not a gondola to be found. Tables with point-of-sale displays, stands, and an occasional spinner are counter-balanced by quality accessories such as a beautiful grandfather clock, a grand collection of autographs, old school tables, desks, antique furniture, an occasional rolling ladder, and leather-and-cloth upholstered club and wing chairs.

In-store events are a major part of this store's ambiance. Events are nicely described in a monthly bulletin. The first, second and third floors open directly onto a large parking deck. The plan and design by the in-store staff has a natural cadence created by plain, stained-pine shelves against a green carpet and beige background. Lighting is simple and not intrusive. The staff at the Tattered Cover Book Store delights in answering questions, treating each one as a riddle that is fun to solve.

NEW YORK UNIVERSITY PROFESSIONAL BOOKSTORE
New York City, N.Y.

Loft Look For A Graduate Business and Law Store in Greenwich Village

This new bookstore, a stone's throw away from the Main NYU campus, is one of New York's leading specialist academic and professional booksellers.

While academics debate the latest theories in the aisles and politicians and business people ponder the alternatives in the 1993 section, visiting students from all over the world gather together their texts and recommended reading materials and head to this lively and spacious ground floor shop with a truly international atmosphere. Joanne McGreevy directs an experienced staff that helps guide customers through the tens of thousands of titles continually held in stock, featuring the most recent and important titles in the fields of graduate business, law and related disciplines.

ABOVE L: The original bottle-glass skylight was saved, restored and featured in the renovation. BELOW L: The "loft" look of the space - exposed structure, partial brick walls and wood floors - were integrated into the merchandising concept. OPPOSITE PAGE: Classical signage, gold leaf treatment on the show windows, a box-type awning canopy, new doors, and a traditional color scheme were combined to create this new storefront, which lives in peace with neighborhood stores.

UNIVERSITY BOOKSTORE
Hilldale Shopping Mall, Madison, Wis.
A General Independent Bookstore

A book buyer's oasis in a midwestern city with a high percentage of readers, this is a comprehensive and well-stocked bookshop with a range that caters to every taste.

As the largest bookstore in Madison, this branch of the University Bookstore was recently repositioned, remerchandised and reimaged with a classical green, black and gold color scheme. Services and POS capability were expanded. An interactive ROM-CD information feature was added. The store stocks a number of specialty book categories, including business books, computer and reference books, science fiction and literature.

There is a good range of services and a good selection of magazines, journals and newspapers; books on tape and language cassettes are also available.

THE BOOK NOOK
Wyckoff, N.J.

A General Independent Bookstore That Expanded

Husband-and-wife team John and Betty Bennett operate this neat store. This small general bookshop aims to stock the major reviewed titles in hardback and paperback and holds a good general back stock. There is a wonderful, separate children's section. The store has been a success, doubling its size after just two years of operation.

The store is well-arranged. The selection and services are outstanding. It has a knack for keeping popular, hard-to-find books in stock. Special orders, author readings and signings, and advertising for out-of-print book requests are part of the services. The mauve and gray color scheme is balanced by custom oak fixtures. Customers particularly like its fast special-order services.

CANTERBURY
BOOKSELLERS
COFFEEHOUSE
Madison, Wis.

A General Independent Bookstore Coffeehouse

This bookselling concept combines the comforts of home - as customers browse the shelves - with the pleasure of taste - they may sample the fare.

Trudy Barash is the creative energy behind this relaxing store. The dark, muted walls are accented by bright book corners, with soft lights chasing shadows around rich case work. Classical music and cushioned sofas invite customers to select any one of the 40,000 titles regularly stocked, or peruse them before purchasing.

This wonderful store, with a quality staff, is an asset to the community.

VISITORS CENTER BOOKSTORE
Gettysburg National Military Park
Historic Site - Specialty Bookshop

Located in sight of the place where Abraham Lincoln made his famous Gettysburg Address, this Eastern National Bookshop features maps, prints, reproductions, reference and related general titles. Selections include biographies, books on badges, medals and uniforms, and regimental and campaign histories relating to the civil war and the action that took place at Gettysburg in particular. The store also features a small but convenient children's section. Before leaving, visitors can further their knowledge of the civil war by buying books and maps here in this friendly shop. The service is outstanding.

ACADEMY BOOKSTORE
U.S. Military Academy, West Point, N.Y.
A General Independent Academic Bookstore

This is a "campus neighborhood store" where cadets can charge books to their account. The staff is helpful and knowledgeable. It has a knack for keeping popular "West Point Bestsellers" and hard-to-find books in stock. Magazines, periodicals and journals, fiction, literature, military history, computer science and technology sections are provided. The store has a wide-open front, central cashier and is clearly marked with tasteful category signs and appropriate graphics. The stock, about 15,000 titles, is kept up well.

THE BOOK ROOM
University of Toronto, Ontario, Canada
A Large General Academic Bookstore

This former metro library reading room was saved and remodeled into a world-class super bookstore. Classical details used in the design of case work relate to the neo-classic/Renaissance influences of the ceiling. The space is bordered on two sides by raised galleries and accessed by customer-service ramps and stairs. The change in height resulted in taller bookcases on the lower level and greater book capacity. The color palette - oak parquet and rich green carpet floor covering, red oak case work and the ceiling colors - is accented with colorful flags and banners.

Beyond its book offerings, THE BOOK ROOM offers text and reference books, a computer store, academic supplies and campus lifestyle merchandise departments.

The staff is always willing to offer advice and further information on specific titles. They are proud of their reputation for providing an efficient and speedy special-order service. Browsing in THE BOOK ROOM can be productive and satisfying. This is a world-class bookstore by any definition.

GALLERIA BOOKSTORE
Galleria Shopping Mall, Atlanta, Ga.

An Upscale General Independent Bookstore

The client envisioned an upscale bookstore, with an updated image. A cohesive concept was created out of four areas with distinct personalities and needs: an entrance sales room leading to a central sales room with raised galleries; the Business Bureau, a professional book department; and the back room and offices to support the store. RIGHT: Classical details added to light coves and column treatments set a rich, upscale atmosphere. BELOW: Raised galleries, beige travatine marble, toast-colored carpet, brass handrails and fruitwood finishes on oak case work were combined in this contextural bookstore design concept.

UNIVERSITY STORE-
STUDENT SERVICES, INC.
Millersville University, Millersville, Pa.
A General University Bookstore

Located on two floors of a new, 10,000-square-foot addition to the Student Union, these educational booksellers have expert staff on hand to guide customers, students in particular, through their extensive range of text, reference and trade titles.

Special sections of the store include art and school supplies, a large range of cassettes and CDs, campus wear, lifestyle merchandise, cards, gifts, computers, study aids and a well-run, comprehensive copy shop. The service is friendly, helpful and attentive.

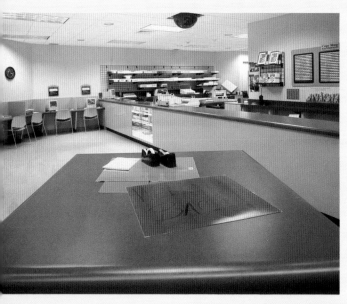

ABOVE: Gift department. CENTER: Copy shop. BELOW: Suspended graphic system in the textbook department.

PACIFIC STARS & STRIPES BOOKSTORE
Osan A.F. Base, Korea

An Independent General Bookstore

This is a nice neighborhood store. It was primarily designed for use by the Air Force personnel and their dependents, in-transit personnel and authorized visitors to the base. The store stocks 20,000 titles, a large selection of magazines and newspapers, and offers many well-used services. The floor is practical vinyl tile, the fixtures oak and the main light source is fluorescent. This was the first "turnkey" bookstore we designed, built and installed in the Far East. We planned, designed, procured and provided logistical support and onsite coordination for these many stores.

PACIFIC STARS & STRIPES BOOKSTORE
U.S. Naval Base, Yokosuka, Japan
A General Independent Bookstore

Schedule played an important part in the design of all Pacific Stars & Stripes bookstores.

They were planned and designed in Westwood, N.J., built in West New York, shipped by rail/container to Seattle, by sea to Yohohama and, finally, carried overland by truck to their destination.

Typically the containers were unloaded at 8:00 a.m. on Monday morning. We worked 14-hour days installing store fixtures, hanging signs, and getting the store fully stocked and ready to cut the ribbon, slice the cake and open for business the following Monday morning at 10:00 a.m. Once you complete a project like this, you have the feeling you have created something that people will use and enjoy.

HSU BOOKSTORE
Humboldt State University, Arcata, Calif.

A General University Bookstore

A bright, cheerful college store of approximately 10,000 square feet, this retail facility is on the second floor of the HSU Student Center building.

There is a well-designed and merchandised general book department offering approximately 15,000 titles. Bestsellers and new titles are displayed; magazines, newspapers and bargain books are also stocked. Other departments include textbooks, computers, clothing, cards, prints, posters, school, office and art supplies, and sundries.

The store features a new college store look - young, crisp and vibrant. There is the bonus of a helpful management and a well-informed staff to meet any customer's request, however small or specialized.

LEFT: Visual merchandise pinata prop was hung on wires from an open ceiling grid by the staff for Mexico theme promotion. Main aisle leads through the book department to maximize customer traffic exposure. BELOW: Theme table set for Halloween promotions.

ABOVE L: "ETC." is a convenience-store boutique in the HSU Bookstore merchandised with white "crib" gondolas, recessed coolers and easy shopping alcoves. ABOVE R: Tracklights highlight campus apparel, cubed, folded and hung on low racks. BELOW L: Clearly visible and well-signed information desk serves general and textbook department. BELOW R: Gifts, posters and specialty cards are merchandised as a "swing" department - moving in after the school-opening rush.

ABOVE L: Built-in wall lighting improves merchandising and makes shopping easier in the HSU Bookstore's art department. ABOVE R: Deep shelves accommodate racks of paints and small art supplies. BELOW L: Open grid merchandisers form transparent departmental dividers and accommodate a wide assortment of merchandise. BELOW R: Computer department is self-contained. Hardware is merchandised on floor cubes. Software and supplies are merchandised on walls and divider fixtures.

CLEMSON UNIVERSITY BOOKSTORE
Clemson, S.C.

A University Express Lobby "C" Store

The Cat Shop is located in a highly trafficked lobby space, one that is in touch with its market.

This freestanding, late-hour shop, and the bookstore are operated under the direction of the Clemson University Department of Business Services.

The goal of the project was to make a underutilized space productive, to create a new image and bring the shop on line at a minimum cost and on a tight time schedule. The concept relied on color, graphics, and modernizing existing fixtures to improve customer acceptance and profitability.

The renovation was a big hit. The reason...an enthusiastic management and helpful staff made it work on time and on budget.

OSU BOOKSTORE
Ohio State University, Columbus, Ohio

A Large University Bookstore

This freestanding, island type service information desk is at the entrance to the general book department of a large 30,000-square-foot university bookstore. General and scholarly books are merchandised in this main store space. The store also features a freestanding express shop, located in the lobby of the building where general, popular and specialty magazines, journals, a section of softbound books, snacks and campus lifestyle merchandise is featured. Each department of the OSU store is distinguished by its own unique character and design.

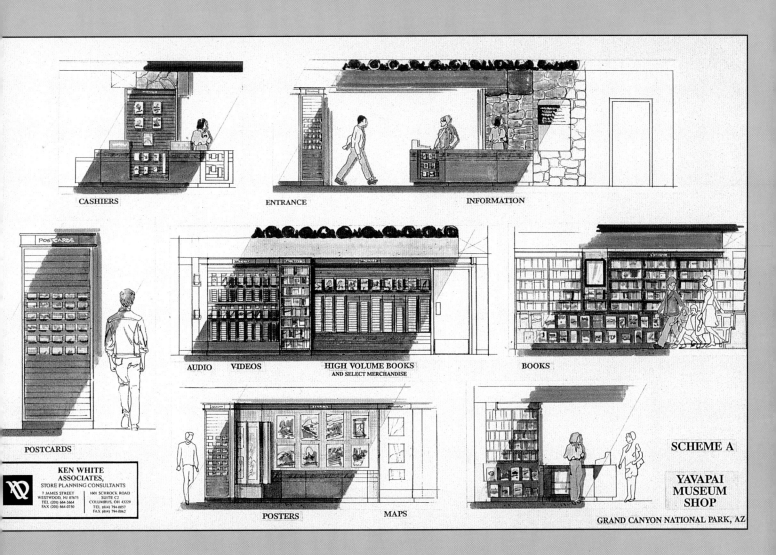

CASHIERS

ENTRANCE

INFORMATION

POSTCARDS

AUDIO VIDEOS

HIGH VOLUME BOOKS
AND SELECT MERCHANDISE

BOOKS

POSTERS

MAPS

SCHEME A

YAVAPAI
MUSEUM
SHOP

GRAND CANYON NATIONAL PARK, AZ

YAVAPAI MUSEUM SHOP
Grand Canyon National Park, Ariz.

A Visitor Information Center Bookshop

Illustrated is the design presentation for a unique bookshop in a small section of a building listed in the historical register, the Yavapai Lookout. The design is simple, with colors chosen to complement the location of the store and provide a nondistracting background for the products presented. Space for a joint-use information desk, multilingual books, maps, audio, video and items relating to the history and geology of the Grand Canyon are featured.

The COMIC STORE OF THE FUTURE will feature comics, graphic novels, newspapers and trip books. It will buy and sell selected collections. The store will have the latest imports from all the major companies and a large selection of back issues. The experiential design will envelop shoppers in a science-fiction fantasy world. Horror, science-fiction-related movie merchandise, plus a wide range of graphic toys, games, model kits and T-shirts, will be featured. To be successful, the shop will carry the most varied stock of any shop of its kind. This presentation, developed for the Comic Expo, visually stated, "We think comic stores should be experiential - a stunning visual experience."

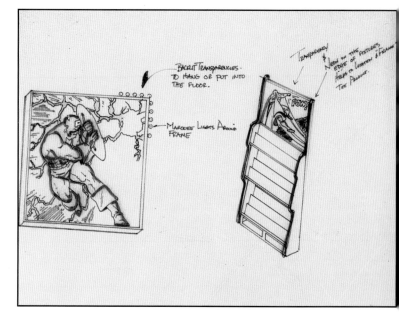

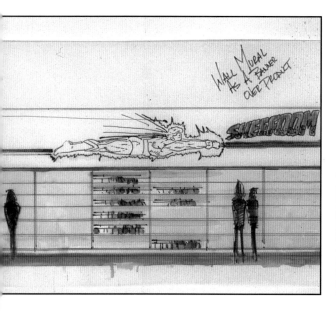

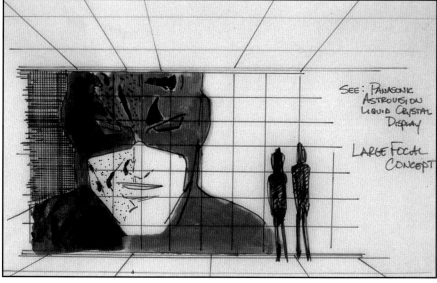

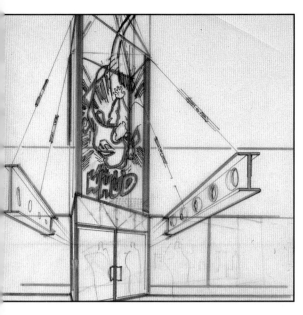

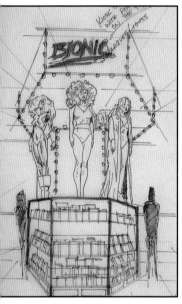

ABOVE L: A storefront entrance with video display and "Gotham City" motifs overhead. ABOVE R: Storefront signs with pulsing neon beams and lighted window frames. FAR R: Another storefront idea. CENTER L: Store fixtures, surrounded by marquee lighting and transparencies of characters. CENTER R: Costume kiosk. Neon graphics with marquee light frame. RIGHT: A key idea of the Comic Expo presentation was 3-dimensional characters with multicolor neon lighting. We thought it would be great for the characters, hung from invisible wires, to simulate a spaz attack. So did Warner Brothers' shops. BELOW L: Neon striping and character wall murals above key products. BELOW CENTER L: Awesome focal concepts - liquid crystal displays reflecting on the floor and ceiling - would add a mind-bending twist to merchandising. BELOW CENTER R: Mannequins in "cool" costumes would help push the comic retail environment to the limit.

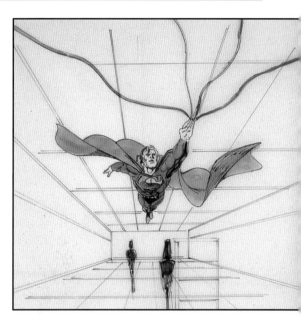

APPENDIX I
Tenant Design Criteria and Requirements

Following is a typical statement provided by many mall managers for tenant use. Although the particulars vary from center to center, the principles remain the same. Individual statements may also include forms to be filled out, which we can help you with.

Introduction

This handbook is to assist the Tenant in the preparation of design, construction, and specifications to meet the requirements of the Landlord and various governing authorities.

This Tenant Handbook and the Tenant Criteria Package should be forwarded to the Tenant's Store Planner as soon as possible. It is essential, because of the magnitude of this project, that the Tenant's Store Planner begin the process of design and working drawings at the earliest possible date. An early submission of drawings for Landlord review and approval could off-set possible delays and extra costs (due to unforeseen trade and material shortages, or premium wages) so that the Tenant's store is completed on time. Should there be any questions after reviewing the information presented in the Tenant Handbook and Criteria Package, contact the Project Manager at the Landlord's office.

Landlord's Project Manager

The role of the Project Manager is to serve as liaison among Landlord, Tenant, Tenant's Store Planner, architect, and Contractor. All plans and correspondence concerning Tenant construction are to be submitted to the Landlord's Project Manager.

Landlord's Field Coordinator

It is the role of the Field Coordinator to provide the Tenant's Store Planner and Contractor with an on-site liaison. Prior to commencing construction, the Tenant's Contractor must check in with the Field Coordinator to obtain a list of rules and regulations, to coordinate activities such as the floor-slab pour and subsequent installation of party-wall studs, and to review the Landlord's approved working drawings filed on site. A close working relationship between the Field Coordinator and the Tenant's General Contractor is essential in order to maintain an orderly progression of work.

Governing Agency

Contact the Building Department code official at the local governing agency. The name and address may be found in your local telephone book. Drawings must conform to all applicable local and national codes. Local building officials should be contacted to find out what codes apply to the building of your store.

TENANT DESIGN CRITERIA
(All work is to be performed by Tenant unless otherwise noted.)

I. ARCHITECTURAL WORK AND FINISHES

A. Floors

1. All slabs on grade shall be a minimum 4" thick with a minimum strength of 3,000 psi with 6 x 6 no. 10 woven wire mesh. Tenant shall provide additional sand-fill and/or remove excess as required, compact 95% modified proctor, and install a vapor barrier of a minimum .004 mill visqueen.

2. Supported floor slabs shall conform with Landlord's project details, and Landlord's design load of 75 lbs per sq. ft.

3. Tenant's finish-floor elevation at storefront shall match Landlord's finish-floor elevation.

4. All exposed concrete must have sealant application.

5. All upper-level Tenant spaces whose use requires wet mopping or is subject to water or other liquids on the floor, and all upper-level toilet rooms shall be provided with an approved membrane waterproofing between Landlord's structural subfloor and Tenant's concrete topping. Such waterproofing shall be installed in such a manner as to prevent the passage of liquids through the floor into the space below.

B. Storefront

1. No element of storefront shall project beyond Tenant's storefront.

2. The design configuration of storefront shall follow the established configuration of the storefront lease line.

3. Materials employed in Tenant's storefront shall be hard-surface, durable materials and shall be selected so as to require minimum maintenance.

4. All storefront work requiring structural support shall be supported at head sections by a welded structural steel framework, which in turn will be securely braced to the existing building's steel structure.

5. All extruded aluminum, used in conjunction with Tenant's storefront, that is exposed while the store is in operation shall have an anodized finish.

6. Storefront grilles or doors shall be stored in a closed pocket during shopping center hours.

7. All mechanical devices (time clocks, grille locks, grille controls, etc.) shall be concealed within Tenant's storefront construction.

8. Electronic surveillance or detection devices shall be incorporated into Tenant's storefront designs and approved by Landlord as part of the working drawing submittal.

C. Walls, Partitions, and Separations

1. Landlord shall erect metal-stud partitions dividing Tenant's lease premises from adjacent Tenants or common areas after placement of Tenant's floor slab or topping.

NOTE: Tenant shall verify Landlord's placement of wall studs and advise Landlord of discrepancies immediately. Failure of Tenant to notify Landlord of discrepancies shall be deemed as acceptance by Tenant and Tenant shall be responsible thereafter.

2. Dividing walls and steel columns shall receive 5/8" fire-code gypsum wallboard with taped and spackled joints from floor to underside of structure above.

3. Tenant's interior partitions shall be made of metal-stud framing with gypsum board finish on all sides, with taped and spackled joints.

4. Tenant shall provide and install noncombustible fire stops as may be required at separations from Tenant's lease space to adjacent areas.

D. Service/Exit Doors

1. Service/exit doors shall be 3' - 0" x 7' - 0" x 1 3/4" hollow metal door, frame, and hardware, all in accordance with governing codes.

2. After installation of service/exit door, Tenant shall restore service corridor to original condition.

3. Service/exit door shall be finished and painted a color specified by Landlord.

E. Ceilings

1. Ceiling heights shall not exceed height indicated on space layout drawing.

2. Ceilings at storefront entry and underside of soffit shall be drywall.

3. In store areas accessible to the public, ceilings shall be sculptured finish 2' x 2' lay-in with recessed T-grid.

NOTE: Tenant may designate certain areas with an exposed structure to execute unique interior design treatments. This option must be discussed and approved by the Project Manager prior to implementing design drawings.

4. All stockrooms or non-public spaces must have 2' x 4' lay-in type ceilings bearing ULI classification markings.

5. Metal suspension systems shall be used for all ceilings.

6. No combustible materials of any sort may be used or stored above Tenant's ceilings.

F. Floor Covering

1. No vinyl or vinyl asbestos tile is permitted in areas accessible to the public.

2. All on-grade floor finishes shall be at the same finish-floor elevation as Landlord's finish-floor elevation at Tenant's storefront.

3. Carpet strips at material transitions are prohibited.

G. Interiors

1. Toilet rooms shall have sanitary floors, base, and threshold, and shall be watertight.

2. Rubbish storage rooms shall be provided in all food- or beverage-service Tenant areas.

3. Audio systems installed by Tenant shall be designed such that sound will be contained within Tenant's lease premises. No speaker or sound-emitting device shall be installed or employed within 20 feet of Tenant's storefront lease line and shall be directed toward the interior of the space.

4. Cash wrap areas shall be no closer than 20 feet from the Tenant's storefront lease line.

II. GRAPHICS

A. Exterior: Permanent Storefront Signage

1. Tenant shall identify his premises with an illuminated sign at the storefront.

2. Only the storefront at the lease premises facing malls and/or courts shall be identified with a sign. Tenant's sign shall be subject to the following requirements and limitations:

    a. Sign letters shall be metal sided, plastic face, trim caps, and mounted directly on sign fascia panels.

    b. The average height of sign letters or components shall not exceed 14".

    c. No part of the sign letters shall hang free of the background.

    d. Sign shall not project beyond the lease line of the lease premises more than 2" inches if less than 8' feet above finish-floor line, or more than 6" above 8' feet.

    e. Signs shall be limited to the store name only; reference to specific merchandise or activity is prohibited.

    f. Sign letters or components shall not have exposed neon or other lamps. All light sources shall be concealed by translucent material. Surface brightness of translucent material shall be consistent in all letters and components of the sign.

    g. The extreme outer limits of the sign letters, components, or insignia shall fall within a rectangle, the two short sides of which shall not fall closer than 24" to the side lease line of the premises, and the top side of which shall fall no closer than 12" to the soffit of the mall fascia element.

    h. The use of corporate shields, crests, logos, or insignias will be permitted (subject to Landlord's approval) provided such corporate shields, crests, logos, or insignias shall not exceed the average height for sign letters.

3. Prohibited types of signs or sign components are as follows:

    a. Signs employing flashing lights.

    b. Signs employing exposed raceways, ballast boxes, or transformers.

    c. Signs exhibiting the name, stamps, or decals of sign manufacturers or installers.

    d. Signs employing painted and/or non-illuminated letters.

    e. Signs employing luminous vacuum-formed plastic letters.

    f. Shadow-box type signs.

    g. Signs employing unedged or uncapped plastic letters with no returns or exposed fastenings.

    h. Rooftop signs.

    i. Signs of box or cabinet type, employing transparent, translucent, or luminous plastic background panels are subject to Landlord's special approval.

B. Interior Graphics

No signage, temporary or permanent, illuminated or non-illuminated, will be permitted within 10' of the storefront lease line without prior written approval of the Landlord. Tenant shall submit, with working drawings, plans indicating the locations, details for display, credit card notices, or other forms of merchandising signage to be posted at or near Tenant's storefront for Landlord's approval. Landlord reserves the right to require the removal, or cause to be removed, any storefront signage not previously approved by Landlord.

1. Graphics prohibited are as follows: Paper, plastic, and cardboard signs; stickers; and silverleaf, goldleaf, or any other kind of decals hung around, on, or behind storefront glass or within storefront space.

2. Graphics permitted are as follows: Back-illuminated signs and graphics.

NOTE: The service door of the leased premises shall be identified with a plastic sign uniform for all Tenants in accordance with Standard Project Details.

III. STRUCTURAL WORK

Any alterations and/or additions and reinforcements to Landlord's structure to accommodate Tenant's work shall be subject to prior written approval of Landlord. Tenant shall leave Landlord's structure as strong or stronger than the original design, with finishes unimpaired.

Concrete floor penetrations required by Tenant shall be installed in accordance with Standard Project Details and engineered to accommodate existing conditions. All floor penetrations in upper-level food- or beverage-service Tenant areas and all toilet rooms shall have watertight sleeves extending a minimum of 4" above finish floor. (See Landlord's Standard Project Detail.)

Roof repairs required by Tenant's cutting of roof and deck material and the repair of same shall be performed by Landlord's roofing contractor at Tenant's expense. Tenant shall enter into a direct contract with Landlord's roofing contractor.

Structural supports and curbing required for openings will be provided by Tenant in accordance with Standard Project Details at Tenant's expense, prior to cutting roof.

IV. HEATING, VENTILATING, AND AIR CONDITIONING

A. Landlord's Work

Landlord, on behalf of Tenant, shall prepare design and working drawings and specifications for, and shall initially construct and/or provide the following:
1. A series of variable-volume roof-top air conditioning units completely installed, including "economizer" option.
2. Space-conditioned, filtered, fixed-temperature, variable-volume air through a series of vertical duct shafts and horizontal supply ducts.
3. Conventional high-velocity supply ducts stubbed into, or in close proximity to, each Tenant space at a point which is nearest to Landlord's distribution system.
4. Landlord will provide project-standard variable air volume control device sets (at Tenant's expense), complete with thermostats. VAV control device sets will be on the job site for delivery to and installation by Tenant's Contractor.

5. Return air will be taken above retail space and mall ceilings. Landlord will provide screened openings above ceiling in Tenant's demising walls for passage of return air. Size and location to be determined by Landlord.
6. Toilet exhaust system including toilet exhaust ducts stubbed into, or in close proximity to, each Tenant space at a point nearest to Landlord's distribution system.
7. The air conditioning supply system, as provided by the Landlord, will be designed and installed for the following conditions in the sales areas only:
    a. To maintain an inside temperature of 76° F plus or minus 2° F db and 50 percent plus or minus rh during summertime.
    b. When outside conditions are 94° F db and 78° F wb and the following inside design conditions are not exceeded:
        1) Lighting: 6.0 Watts per square foot
        2) Occupancy: One person per 75 square feet

B. Tenant's Work

Tenant, at his or her sole cost and expense, shall prepare design and working drawings and specifications for and shall initially construct and/or provide the following:
1. All heating, ventilation, and exhaust equipment and controls, ducts, insulation, and all structural, plumbing, and electrical work related thereto. Tenant shall provide his own individual system proceeding from the low-velocity air conditioning ducts provided for him and the toilet exhaust duct provided for him. All equipment shall bear the U.L. label.
2. Air Conditioning
    a. Tenant shall furnish and install a minimum of one VAV control device set. Units shall have a capability to adjust in the field from 0 to 100 percent of minimum air flow (normally set at 20 percent minimum). Discharge air volume from units shall not be affected by the upstream duct pressure variations. Units shall be insulated to minimize noise to the space. Variable volume terminal units may be controlled by solid state electronic, electric, or duct-pressure power motors and space thermostats.

    b. Tenant shall furnish a standard low-velocity air distribution system to sales and/or dining areas of Tenant space. Tenant, at his discretion, may elect to supply air to other than sales areas with the understanding that temperatures, as stated above, may not be maintained.
    c. Ductwork shall be fabricated of galvanized sheet metal per American Society of Heating, Refrigeration, and Air Conditioning Engineers' standards as outlined for low-pressure ducts in the latest edition of the *Guide and Data Book*.
    d. Tenant's supply ductwork may be insulated, and all ductwork shall be installed in concealed space above ceilings.
    e. Quantity of air supplied to Tenant's space will be verified by Landlord upon review of Tenant's working drawings.

NOTE: Clear access shall be provided to all equipment.

3. Heating
    a. The major portion of required Tenant heating will be generated by inherent internal loads, that is, the daytime contribution made by people and lighting.
    b. Those Tenants affected by heat losses (roof, external walls, doors, windows, etc.) shall install independent electric heat, fed from Tenants' power source, consisting of the following:
        1) Roof. By self-contained thermostatically controlled electric unit heaters installed in the space between ceiling and roof. Unit heaters shall be designed to maintain a minimum inside dry bulb temperature of 55° F in this plenum. Thermostat for same shall be set and locked at 55° F.
        2) Exterior walls, doors, windows, etc. By self-contained, thermostatically controlled electric unit heaters and/or electric baseboard type radiant heaters. Heaters shall be designed to maintain minimum inside dry-bulb temperature of 70° F in affected space.

4. Ventilation

a. Central air conditioning supply system will provide minimum air circulation of 7.5 CFM outside air per occupant. Outside air provided for sales and/or dining areas only.

b. Toilet rooms shall be exhausted per code. Exhausters shall be of ceiling or in-line type complete with backdraft damper and duct connection to Landlord's toilet exhaust system.

5. Standard Design Criteria shall be as follows:

a. Central air conditioning system will provide 55° F plus 2° F air with outside temperature at 94° F db and 78° F wb.

b. Tenant's heating equipment shall be designed to maintain previously defined minimum inside dry-bulb temperatures when outside temperature is 12° F db, and average wind velocity is 15 MPH.

NOTE: Landlord's central air conditioning supply system will not operate during shopping center off-hours, as determined by Landlord.

6. Nonstandard Tenant Requirements shall be as follows:

a. Tenant shall provide all process requirements, hood exhausts, make-up air supplies, equipment vents, and other contaminated exhausts. When permitted by Landlord, they shall extend in ductwork through the roof. This ductwork, serving lower level Tenants, shall be located in special shafts, built by Tenant at location and of construction designated by the Landlord.

b. All process exhausts, hood exhausts, equipment vents, and other contaminated exhausts, when permitted by Landlord, shall discharge vertically to the atmosphere 20'-0" minimum horizontally away from any fresh-air intakes, properly dispersing odors or fumes away from same.

c. Nonstandard Tenant roof equipment shall be located in areas designated by the Landlord to specified heights and in accordance with Landlord's standard details for equipment on the roof.

1) Should weight or location of equipment by Tenant require supports, screens, cat walks, or roof hatch and ladder, they shall be provided by Tenant in accordance with standard details. Landlord shall determine when and where the above shall be required.

2) All above equipment shall be finish-painted in accordance with the Landlord's paint schedule and specifications.

3) Tenant's roof equipment shall be clearly identified with Tenant's name.

NOTE: It is suggested that each nonstandard Tenant's HVAC design be submitted to Landlord on a preliminary basis, prior to preparation of working drawings.

V. PLUMBING

A. Landlord's Work

1. On-site water supply mains for domestic and fire protection, shut-off valves, and fire hydrants. Interior domestic water branch lines stubbed above or below Tenant's lease premises at a point to be determined by Landlord.

2. Sanitary and plumbing vent branch lines stubbed above or below.

B. Tenant's Work

1. Plumbing fixtures and distribution systems, including all rough-in and final connections for same. Hot and insulated cold water lines, drains and vents, electrical hot-water heaters, and complete installation of and final connections to Tenant's specialty equipment.

2. Plumbing fixtures and accessories shall be of commercial quality and shall be of water conserving type.

3. Food-and-beverage-service Tenants shall provide cast-iron grease traps located within leased premises.

4. Floor drains shall be provided in toilet rooms and kitchens.

5. Pipe sleeves shall be installed in penetrations through upper-level floor slabs.

VI. FIRE PROTECTION

A. Landlord's Work

1. Interior hydraulically-calculated fire protection sprinkler system main stubbed above Tenant's premises at a point to be

determined by Landlord. Fire protection system shall be provided with a supervised alarm system.

B. Tenant's Work

1. Hydraulically calculated fire protection sprinkler system, fire hose cabinets, fire extinguishers, and other equipment within Tenant's leased premises in accordance with Landlord's insurance underwriters' Fire Rating Inspection Bureau, and code requirements. Since the entire fire protection system for the project is required to be an interrelated, centrally-controlled installation, Tenant shall cause to be designed and installed, by a qualified sprinkler contractor, said system within Tenant's lease premises in accordance with the Landlord's review, shop drawings, specifications, and hydraulic calculations for the sprinkler system that have been approved by the Fire Rating Inspection Bureau. Landlord's approval of the foregoing shall not constitute the assumption of any responsibilities by Landlord for the accuracy or sufficiency thereof, and Tenant shall be solely responsible thereafter.

VII. ELECTRICAL WORK

A. Landlord's Work

1. Electrical primary and secondary distribution systems. Electrical secondary distribution system with service feeder will terminate in a check meter in Tenant's leased premises at a point to be determined by Landlord. Electrical service to the Tenant's premises shall consist of the following voltage: 277/480 volt, 3 phase, 4 wire, 60 cycle.

2. Telephone incoming feeders to project central distribution, at locations designated by Landlord. Branch system conduit to Tenant's leased premises by Tenant.

B. Tenant's Work

1. Tap box, panelboard(s), transformer(s), distribution center, conduits, and all branch wiring, outlet boxes, and final connections to all electrical devices including mechanical equipment, controls, and signs.

2. All lighting fixtures, lamps, convenience outlets, time clocks, signs, and all related conduits and wiring.

3. Telephone equipment, conduits, and wire from central distribution point outside the leased premises to and within the leased premises, and related items for same.

4. Television and burglar alarm equipment and all conduits, wiring, and related items for same. The installation of any roof-mounted antenna must be approved, in writing, by Landlord.

5. Internally illuminated exit and emergency lighting as required by governing codes.

6. Transformers, ballast, conduit, wiring, and related items for signs.

7. Service call system. Tenant shall provide and install a buzzer call system and all related conduit and wire.

8. All equipment shall bear Underwriter Laboratories, Inc. label.

9. Three phase transformers (dry type) provided by all Tenants shall have six standard full-capacity tap arrangements. Entire installation within Tenant's premises shall be balanced equally across all three phases.

10. Entire installation shall meet all requirements of national and/or local electrical codes.

11. Audio systems installed by Tenant shall be designed such that sound shall be contained within Tenant's leased premises. No speaker or sound-emitting device shall be installed or employed within twenty feet of Tenant's storefront lease line and shall be directed toward the interior of the space.

VIII. PROCEDURES FOR PREPARATION OF PLANS AND SPECIFICATIONS FOR APPROVAL

The following sections define the legal responsibilities of both Tenant and Landlord. An understanding of these sections by the Tenant and his Store Planner is essential before any attempt is made to start design or construction.

A. Design Drawings

1. The Tenant has been provided with a design criteria package. Included in this package will be the following:

a. A sheet of standard project details.

b. A delineation of the actual space the Tenant will occupy. It will be the responsibility of the Tenant and/or his Store Planner to field-verify all conditions and dimensions pertaining to same. Any exception taken to this information indicated on the drawing should be brought to the attention of the Landlord immediately.

2. Within thirty days from either of the following dates, whichever shall be later to occur: (a) receipt by Tenant of space layout drawings, or (b) execution of the lease by Landlord and Tenant, Tenant shall submit to the Landlord for review and approval, one set of prints and one set of reproducible prints of store design drawings.

3. After review of store design drawings, Landlord shall return to Tenant one set of prints of store design drawings with his modification, approval, or disapproval.

4. If store design drawings are returned to Tenant not bearing the Landlord's approval, said store design drawings shall be immediately revised by Tenant and resubmitted to Landlord for approval within ten days of their receipt by Tenant.

5. Any revision of the approved design drawings must be approved in writing by the Landlord prior to its implementation.

B. Working Drawings and Specifications

1. The Tenant shall engage a Store Planner registered in the state of the project location for the purpose of preparing working drawings and specifications for the Tenant's lease premises.

2. Working drawings and specifications shall be due in the Landlord's office within 21 days from receipt by Tenant of Landlord's approval of store design drawings.

3. Such drawings shall be submitted to Landlord for his approval in the form of one set of prints, and one set of reproducible prints (sepias).

4. *Schedule of Drawings.* Working drawings, to the minimum scale as called below, and specifications shall include but not be limited to the following:

a. Format size to be 30" x 42".

b. Key plan showing location of leased premises.

c. Floor plan at minimum scale of 1/8" x 1'-0".

d. Overall sections at 1/8" scale.

e. Reflected ceiling plan at 1/8" scale.

f. Plan, elevation, and sections of storefront at 1/4" scale.

g. Interior elevations at 1/8" scale.

h. Full sections of types of partitions used at 1/2" scale.

i. Details of special conditions encountered at 1 1/1" scale, including applicable Landlord typical details (i.e., neutral pier, and roof openings).

j. Storefront completely detailed at 1 1/2" scale.

k. Door schedule with jamb details at 1 1/2" scale.

l. Finish and color schedule.

m. Sprinkler, plumbing, heating, ventilating, and cooling plans at 1/8" scale.

n. Mechanical plans and final mechanical load calculations.

NOTE: Mechanical drawings will not be reviewed without complete mechanical load tabulation form.

o. Mechanical details at 1/4" scale.

p. Electrical details, fixturing schedules, one-line electrical riser diagram, and final electrical load tabulations.

NOTE: Electrical drawings will not be reviewed without complete electrical load tabulation form.

q. Specifications covering all of Tenant's work: architectural (including list of hardware), electrical, plumbing, heating, ventilating, and air conditioning.

5. Drawings must conform to all local and national codes and regulations.

6. After review of Tenant's working drawings, Landlord shall return to the Tenant one set of prints of the working drawings with his modifications, approval, or disapproval.

7. If working drawings are returned to the Tenant not bearing Landlord's approval, said working drawings shall be immediately revised by the Tenant and resubmitted to Landlord for approval within ten days of their receipt by Tenant.

IX. PROCEDURE AND REQUIREMENTS FOR CONSTRUCTION OF THE LEASED PREMISES BY TENANT

A. Commencing Construction

1. The Tenant shall be required to commence construction not later than twenty-one days after receipt by the Tenant of approved working drawings by Landlord or from date of written notice by Landlord that the Tenant's premises are ready for construction.

B. General Requirements

1. The Tenant may not commence construction until all of the following items have been completed:

   a. The Tenant has received a fully executed lease from the Landlord.
   b. The Tenant has received approval for working drawings from the Landlord.

2. Tenant has submitted to Landlord the following information:

   a. The names and addresses of the general, mechanical, and electrical contractors Tenant intends to engage in the construction of his lease premises.
   b. The date on which the Tenant's construction work will commence, together with the estimated date of completion of Tenant's construction and fixturing work, and date of Tenant's projected opening for business in the lease premises.
   c. Estimated construction costs, including architectural, engineering, and contractors' fees.
   d. Tenant's contractors' performance and/or labor and material bonds, if so required by the Landlord, or any other bond to be furnished by the Tenant as may be required by Landlord to insure the faithful performance of the work in accordance with the drawings and specifications approved by the Landlord.

3. Tenant's General Contractor shall contact Landlord's Field Coordinator to coordinate his plans with Landlord's approved drawings.

4. The Tenant has submitted to Landlord evidence of insurance as outlined below.

X. INSURANCE

Tenant shall secure, pay for, and maintain, or cause his contractors to secure, pay for, and maintain, during construction and fixturing work within lease premises, all of the insurance policies required and in the amounts set forth herein. Tenant shall not permit his contractors to commence any work until all required insurance has been obtained and certificates of such insurance have been delivered to Landlord.

A. Tenant's General Contractor's and Sub-Contractors' Required Minimum Coverage and Limits of Liability.

1. Workmen's compensation, as required by state law, and including employer's liability insurance with a limit of not less than $2,000,000 and any insurance required by any employee benefits acts or other statutes applicable where the work is to be performed as will protect the contractor and sub-contractors from any and all liability under the aforementioned acts.

2. Comprehensive general liability insurance (including Contractor's protective liability) in an amount not less than $2,000,000 for any one occurrence whether involving bodily injury liability (or death resulting therefrom) or property damage liability or a combination thereof with an aggregate limit of $2,000,000. Such insurance shall provide for explosion, collapse, and underground coverage. Such insurance shall insure Tenant's General Contractor against any and all claims for bodily injury, including death resulting therefrom and damage to or destruction of property of any kind whatsoever and belonging to whomever and arising from his operations under the contract and whether such operations are performed by Tenant's General Contractor, subcontractors, or any of their subcontractors, or by anyone directly or indirectly employed by any of them.

3. Comprehensive automobile liability insurance, including the ownership, maintenance, and operation of any automotive equipment, owned, hired, and non-owned in the following amounts:

   a. Bodily injury, per occurrence for personal injury and/or death: $2,000,000.

   b. Property damage liability: $2,000,000. Such insurance shall insure the General Contractor and/or subcontractors against any and all claims for bodily injury, including death resulting therefrom and damage to property of others caused by accident and arising from their operations under contract, whether such operations are performed by the General Contractor, subcontractors, or by anyone directly or indirectly employed by any of them.

B. Tenant's Protective Liability Insurance

1. Tenant shall provide owner's protective liability insurance as will insure Tenant against any and all liability to third parties for damages because of bodily injury liability (or death resulting therefrom) and property damage liability of others or a combination thereof which may arise from work in connection with the lease premises, and any other liability for damages which Tenant's General Contractor and/or subcontractors are required to insure against under any provisions herein. Said insurance shall be provided in the minimum amount of $2,000,000.

C. Tenant's Builders' Completed Value Builders' Risk Material Damage Insurance Coverage

1. Tenant shall provide an "All Physical Loss" builders' risk insurance policy on the work to be performed for Tenant in the leased premises as it relates to the building within which the lease premises is located. The policy shall include as insured the Tenant, his contractors and subcontractors, and Landlord, as their interests may appear. The amount of insurance to be provided shall be 100% of the replacement cost.

XI. PROCEDURE, SCHEDULES, AND OBLIGATIONS BY THE TENANT FOR THE CONSTRUCTION OF THE PREMISES

A. Tenant's General Contractor

1. All contractors engaged by Tenant shall be bondable, licensed contractors, possessing good labor relations, capable of performing quality workmanship, and working in harmony with Landlord's General Contractor and other contractors on the job. All work shall be coordinated with general project work.

B. Construction Procedures

1. General Rules

a. Construction shall comply in all respects with applicable federal, state, county and/or city statutes, ordinances, regulations, laws, and codes. All required building and other permits in connection with the construction and completion of the lease premises shall be obtained and paid for by the Tenant.

b. Tenant shall apply for and pay for all utility services.

c. Tenant shall cause his Contractor to provide warranties for not less than one year against defects in workmanship and equipment.

d. Tenant's work shall be subject to the inspection of Landlord, his consultants, and his supervisory personnel.

e. Tenant shall pay for all temporary utility facilities, and the removal of debris, as necessary and required in connection with the construction of the leased premises. Storage of Tenant's contractors' construction material, tools, equipment, and debris shall be confined to the lease premises and in the areas which may be designated for such purposes by Landlord. In no event shall any material or debris be stored in the mall or service/exit corridors.

NOTE: If debris is found in these areas, it will be removed at the expense of the Tenant who is responsible.

f. During construction, Landlord will provide temporary electrical service in an area designated by the Landlord. Tenant shall request permission to connect temporary lines in the power source for service to his premises.

g. During initial construction, Tenant fixturing, and merchandise stocking, Landlord will provide trash removal service from designated truck court areas. At any time, as determined by Landlord, Landlord may discontinue trash removal service and Tenant shall assume responsibility therefor. All such work shall be performed by contractors approved by the Landlord.

h. Tenant's General Contractor shall inform Landlord's Engineering Director 24 hours prior to his intention to shut down sprinkler system for purposes of tying into the project system.

i. Tenant must contact the Landlord's roofing contractor to make any penetrations through the Landlord's roof.

j. All roof openings require steel framing, which is to be installed by Tenant's Contractor prior to cutting roof opening.

k. All roof units, fans, and switches shall be labeled with the name and number of Tenant store as soon as it is possible.

l. The metal studs to be installed by Landlord will be installed after the Tenant's slab has been poured. The Tenant who pours his slab first shall pour to the outside of the metal plate that is to be installed for this party wall. The Tenant's Contractor shall make sure that these studs are plumb and evenly spaced prior to installation of drywall.

C. Completion

1. Tenant is responsible for securing a Certificate of Occupancy from governmental authorities.

2. Upon the completion of the Tenant's work, all facilities shall be fully usable for the purpose intended without defects.

3. Upon the completion of the Tenant's work, warranties (one year from date of store opening) on all work and equipment shall be provided to Landlord by Tenant. All warranties relating to mechanical and electrical systems shall be extended to Landlord.

D. Tenant Close-Out Process

1. Within 30 days of opening or at the request of Landlord, whichever is earlier, Tenant shall be responsible to Landlord for the following:

a. Tenant or Tenant's Contractor must have made payment of all construction charges due.

b. The premises must be 100% complete, in accordance with good workmanship and the working drawings and specifications as approved by Landlord.

c. Provide Landlord with a copy of unqualified, final Certificates of Occupancy from the Building Department.

d. Letter from Tenant stating date Tenant is open for business.

e. Letter from Tenant listing the total cost of material and labor by trade for leasehold improvements: Tenant's fixtures and Landlord-furnished work in the premises.

f. Tenant's Affidavit of Inspection and acceptance of the premises.

g. Waiver of lien, with original signatures from Tenant's General Contractor and each subcontractor for the amounts specified in Item No. 5. No partial waivers of lien will be accepted.

h. One set of "as-built" sepias for Landlord's file.

i. Fixture and equipment warranties valid for one year from date Tenant opens for business.

j. Certification of noncombustible lumber, if used, conforming to U. L. requirements.

k. Statement from Tenant wherein Tenant agrees to indemnify Landlord for any claims by material suppliers, contractors, or subcontractors.

l. Execution of an estoppel letter prepared by Landlord.

APPENDIX II
Management Advisory Services

Introduction

Bookstore management advisory services and consulting are, by nature, customized services that are defined by the unique problems and issues faced by individual client booksellers. Let us explain how ours work.

Ken White Associates (KWA) defines its core management advisory consulting expertise as the field of bookstore retailing and retail book distribution. Few firms can match our knowledge and depth of experience in these areas.

Within this realm, KWA Consulting pursues several types of assignments. Our capabilities are strongest in the use of several specific research methodologies. These are used to different degrees and in a variety of ways to provide input on our consulting assignments.

This Appendix lists and describes the services and research methodologies that form the core offering of KWA Management Advisory Services. It is intended to advise and inform booksellers who are not familiar with the professional capabilities of our firm about the outside products in which we specialize and our general approach to consulting assignments.

It is important for us to point out that we are not restricted to the services and methodologies described herein, and that the nature of every assignment varies with the specific issues we are asked to address.

New Bookstore Venture Business Planning

In this process, KWA assists in the development of a total "New Business Package" for booksellers. We include demographic and competitive analyses, mission, market separation, and positioning strategy statements, inventory capacity and cost requirements, category lists, sideline identification and sourcing, buying strategies, store layout, staffing requirements, estimated time and cost-cash flow requirements, proforma statements, sales projections, and marketing strategies.

These elements are crucial to launching a successful prototype retail bookstore business. Your new store is important. KWA can help you develop a custom "New Business Package" to suit your unique situation.

Site and Market Location Analysis

Finding and leasing a retail location to fulfill the economic and image requirements of the store you plan to open is fundamental to its success. The location, image, and appearance of both the store and its neighborhood must appeal to the kind of customers you wish to attract. KWA Site and Market Location Analyses provide a valuable supplement to ABA site location services. In many cases our bookstore merchandise consulting professionals are already familiar with the demographic, competitive, and site factors that may impact your particular concept. We can provide independent and objective advice. Our initial insights are often supplemented by economic statistics and input from you, based on your experiences with the existing locations. We then focus on the particular site or market area being considered to quickly and cost effectively determine your prospects for success at the target location.

Lease Negotiation Service

One of our most popular services is lease negotiation. KWA consultants regularly join clients, their lawyers, and agents to review and sometimes negotiate Canadian and U.S. bookstore leases. Fruitful leases result when booksellers are aware of their strengths and understand the negotiating process, lease language, hidden costs, technical specifications, basic lease provisions, time and build-out allowances, taxes, CAM costs, parking limits, and other tricky items.

On demand, KWA can provide very quick turnaround on professional assessments of lease offers, recommendations for counter-offers, and lease negotiating strategies for each particular situation. KWA also provides on-site input for pressing situations that need to be quickly addressed in an in-depth fashion. If you are about to enter into a lease negotiation or renegotiation, you should seek the advice and counsel of your attorney and an experienced KWA consultant: we can help.

Strategic Independent Superstore Consulting

KWA is the most experienced retail consultant specializing in the planning, design, and merchandising (PDM) of large-scale independent super-bookstores.

KWA provides site location and market and demographic analysis, merchandise planning, and category and department adjacency relationship planning, all of which are critical to the success of super stores. KWA plans POS system integration. We also conceive and design classic image building features for kids', travel, cooking, and other specialty sections: wonderful graphic systems, lighting, and color schemes within strict budgets and time limitations. KWA provides diligent implementation of an entire superstore, a shop within a shop, a graphic system, or a single fixture.

Specialty Bookshop Consulting

KWA provides assistance in developing specialty bookstore and publisher focused concepts: children, cooking, travel, medical, professional, discount, institutional, government, and many others.

KWA helps to weigh costs and benefits, identify requirements and constraints, and develop focused, imaginative, and powerful shop strategies that are exciting to customers and deliver increased performance for booksellers, institutions, agencies, distribution wholesalers, and publishers.

Retail Productivity Enhancement

A key to maximizing bookstore productivity is to justify each merchandise category and evaluate the productivity of the space it consumes. KWA Consulting has developed a unique model for evaluating space, productivity, and allocation adjustments that lead to significant margin and volume enhancements.

KWA's analysis is based on an understanding of both the financial and marketing implications of the title base, inventory levels, gross margins, and merchandise assortment. The end product is a comprehensive report of where the business is, where it can go, and recommendations on how to get there.

Situation Audit and Reaction Strategies

KWA can provide independent booksellers with what-to-do-about-it reaction strategies to counteract encroachment by predator book chains, organizations that enter a market and attempt to "steal" an established bookseller's business.

KWA can survey the situation and provide a professional statement of client bookseller company strategies, plans, and operations versus pending competition.

The outcome of these investigations are specific recommendations to effectively deal with the situation. Recommendations are presented in a report containing ideas for realigning the market focus, increasing market strength, and niche determination, as well as stock and category realignment. Sketch plans, implementation time, and cost estimates are included.

Visual Design and Merchandising Analysis

Visual design and merchandising analysis are valuable for regional chain bookstores, franchises, multi-store organizations, distributors, and wholesalers active in the bookselling business. KWA consultants review elements in a client's most recent prototype for a single bookstore strategy, including an analysis of exterior, storefront, signage, and show window elements.

All classifications of general books, periodicals, and sideline presentations and displays are reviewed and studied for their effect on customers' expectations. Visual presentations highlight a comprehensive written summary of the analysis and findings. The report focuses on strategic, action-oriented recommendations for improvements in the bookstore's image, merchandise presentation and organization, graphics, and layout design.

In-Store Graphics and Communications

Visual communication is the creative leap that sets one bookstore apart from another. KWA designs visuals that will excite and motivate your customers. We excel in bookstore graphic systems, store identity development, seasonal signage, category signs, shelf-talkers, policy and customer service signage, directories, bookmarks, and collateral design. KWA regularly provides cost estimates and designs graphic systems that can be implemented by in-house staff to simplify maintenance and maintain competitive differentiation.

Bookstore Planning, Design, and Merchandising (PDM)

We accomplish the planning, design, and merchandising (PDM) of a wonderful bookstore in four consecutive phases.
Data Collection involves gathering information from you. This will include photos and plans of the space as well as your requirements and wish list.
Planning involves the development of merchandising plans and requirements.
Design is where the image - the look - and style - of the store is created in sketches, renderings, and elevations.
Technical Documentation is systematic and comprehensive.

Our final plans and specifications are sufficient in detail to completely guide the construction and sequencing of the work. KWA can, through it subsidiary, also offer the architectural and engineering services of licensed professionals to carry out special needs. KWA is in a unique position to implement and coordinate execution of the strategies it designs worldwide, from our offices in Columbus, Ohio and Westwood, New Jersey.

GLOSSARY

ABA. American Booksellers Association. A professional organization serving the needs of the bookseller.

AISLE. The space devoted to customer and/or materials circulation within a selling area.

AMBIANCE. The general quality of an interior design representing the store image. (Also called atmosphere.)

ASSORTMENT. A related collection of books displayed by author or subject. May also refer to the overall stock mix in a department or bookstore.

BABY BOOKS. Board books, cloth books, and shaped books intended for children 2 years old and under.

BACKLIST. All titles other than those published within the current season.

BARGAIN BOOKS. The term used by booksellers to describe (1) books sold at a price lower than the original retail price, and (2) books that never had an original price printed on the jacket and are sold at a comparatively low retail price.

BARREL VAULT. A roof or ceiling in the form of continuous, rounded arches.

BESTSELLERS. Titles identified as the result of the compilation and analysis of sales recorded by selected booksellers throughout the country and ranked by *The New York Times* and *Publishers Weekly* on a weekly basis.

BLOCK PLANS. Design drawings showing divisions of the floor plan into block or area adjacencies. Block plans indicate store entrances, stairways, elevators, department locations, stockrooms, service desks, offices, storage space, and other operational elements in the form of blocks.

BOXED SET. A group of series, thematic, subject, or individual-author books or merchandise packaged together in a cardboard carton or in a plastic shrink-wrap cocoon.

BUILDER. The individual, partnership, or corporation that contracts for, organizes, and supervises the construction of a building project.

CASH WRAP. The counter in a bookstore where sales transactions, gift wrapping, and, occasionally, customer service functions take place.

CATEGORY SIGNS. Interchangeable lettered signs, usually made of poster board, indicating the subject matter of display sections in bookstores.

CHECKOUT. A self-selling element designed and located at the exit of an enclosed sales area in a controlled customer traffic pattern. Designed for full-time cashiers and prominently signed.

CIRCULATION PLAN. A plan showing anticipated free customer-flow throughout retail sales areas. Locations of display fixtures are determined by the circulation plan to assure the best merchandise exposure to the greatest number of shoppers.

CLERESTORY. The upper part of a wall that contains windows.

COLOR CONTRASTING. A merchandising technique of arranging books or other merchandise by contrasting their colors to highlight the individual graphic quality of each item. (Also known as coloring out.)

CONTRACT. An agreement, written or verbal, which describes the scope of work to be done and designates the responsibilities of each party.

CONTRACTOR. One who is in charge of an entire store construction project, furnishing the material and labor of one or more trades himself, and employing subcontractors to perform all other necessary work.

COUNTER. A simple selling fixture used for top display and merchandise storage, generally used for over-the-counter selling by sales personnel.

CURTAIN WALL. A partial overhead wall that hangs above the floor on a structural frame. It is sometimes installed above the wallcases in bookstore interiors to give them a custom built-in look.

DANGLER. A promotional sign or device hung overhead from the ceiling.

DECORATING. The planning, composing, and selecting of colors, materials, furniture, furnishings, and accessories to enrich the interior design of a bookstore.

DEMAND SELLING. The concept of presenting merchandise for "must-have" and planned purchases in which location is not a factor.

DEPARTMENT. A section of a retail bookstore stocked with specialized books.

DESIGN. The art of conceptualizing and sketching, in outline, the interior, plan, architecture, equipment, decorating, graphics, and merchandising of a bookstore.

DETAIL DRAWING. A drawing of any small part of a larger unit showing a particular section of the store design, (e.g., a table or gondola).

DOMINANCE. The merchandising posture that visually affirms that the bookstore has the most complete inventory and selection of any bookstore in the community it serves.

DOUBLE-DECK STOCK. Floor and mezzanine stockroom space achieved by the construction of steel shelving to develop the maximum cubic content of high ceiling space.

DROPPED (OR HUNG) CEILING. A ceiling constructed below the main structure or original ceiling, designed to conceal pipes, HVAC ducts, and obstructions; to provide a plane for the placement of an effective lighting system; and to improve the interior proportions.

DUMP DISPLAY. A self-display shipping unit made of cardboard and supplied to bookstores by publishers and manufacturers. Intended to feature from 36 to 45 lead title books and special promotions.

ELEVATION. A scale drawing or design of an interior or exterior element indicating the design, proportions, and finishes of a particular vertical surface.

ESTIMATES. Statements prepared by various contractors and suppliers of buy-out items declaring their charges for providing work and materials described on the plans and in the specifications.

ETAGERE. A modular display fixture suitable for bookstore show window and feature display use, consisting of levels of adjustable glass shelving supported by a polished tubing system.

FACADE. The vertical area or face of a store front, or the face or front part of an interior elevation.

FACE OUT. The display of book titles or other merchandise with the full cover or face design of the book visible and facing the customer.

FIXTURE. Any of various selling devices designed to display, present, and store books and merchandise.

FLOOR PLAN. The specific layout plan of a bookstore, including the arrangement of categories, storefront, walls, aisles, gondolas, tables, racks, etc.

FUNCTIONAL AREA. The building area, including walls, columns, entrances, stairs, escalators, elevators, mechanical equipment and machinery rooms, equipment closets, toilets, ducts, chases, and permanent hallways not available for retail use.

GALLERY. A raised platform constructed of wood or metal onto which sales departments and supervisory offices are placed.

GENERAL BOOKSELLER. A bookseller for whom no one line of books generates more than 50% of sales.

GONDOLA. A center-floor fixture with adjustable and removable wood, metal, or glass shelves, convertible for the display of hanging or folded merchandise.

GONDOLA ENDCAP. Any of several display stands that accommodate single or multiple assortments of books and merchandise at the end of a gondola, generally on the main aisle.

GOTHIC. An architectural style of the Middle Ages (twelfth to sixteenth century) characterized by pointed arches.

GRAPHICS. The combination of visual art techniques applied to bookstore design, including typography and lettering, dimensional background effects, mural painting, and signing of merchandise with price, size, and promotional information.

GROSS BUILDING AREA. Total square footage of space occupied by a bookstore calculated to the outside of the building walls.

HVAC. Heating, ventilating, and air conditioning.

IMPULSE SELLING. The concept of locating merchandise at high-traffic locations in a bookstore to stimulate additional, spur-of-the-moment purchases.

ISLAND. An arrangement of cubes, showcases, counters, and back fixtures to create a visual merchandise sales or display unit.

ISP. Institute of Store Planners, the national organization of professional store planners.

JOBBER. A wholesale merchant who generally specializes in the sale of many classes of consumer goods, including trade and mass-market books, stationery, gifts, pens, art material, film, candy, etc.

LOW TICKET. Low-priced.

L-SHAPED STEPDOWN. A one-piece unit composed of three steps built in an L-shape to fit into or around a corner. Used primarily to feature new arrivals and key titles.

MASS MARKET. A soft cover book of standard size for mass distribution through wholesalers and jobbers to various types of booksellers; a book bought at a straight discount when the publisher has paid the freight and the books are cover return.

MATERIALS HANDLING SYSTEM. The equipment for and methods of receiving, storing, and moving goods from the truck dock to the point of sale within the store.

MERCHANDISING. The buying, administering, presenting, and selling of books and consumer goods at retail to the public, generally for a profit.

MEZZANINE. An area between two floors of a bookstore that is less than half of the floor onto which it is open. (Also called a balcony.)

NET SELLING AREA. The space calculated by subtracting the functional area from the gross area. The remaining space is available for selling to customers and includes fixtured sales areas, stockrooms, fitting rooms, cash wraps, and service desks.

NONSELLING AREA. See *Functional Area*.

OPEN PLANNING. A planning and design concept aimed at achieving a totally open, flexible, visual sales space by the omission of high walls and partitions.

OVERSIZED TITLES. Books that in physical dimensions are larger than normal (i.e., 10 to 12 inches tall or over).

OVERSTOCK. Copies of book titles or merchandise in excess of the shelf stock necessary to meet immediate demand.

OVERSTOCK AREAS. The shelves above the normal wall display space that are used to display overstock.

PARQUET. Flooring composed of wood blocks or strips of a fixed length.

PILASTER. A rectangular column projecting slightly from a wall and designed to simulate a square column with capital, shaft, and base.

POCKET. The space assigned to the display of mass-market titles face out in a rack, dump, gondola, or wall section.

PROGRAM BUDGET. An analytical breakdown of costs of time required to complete a proposed project. Budgets vary from "best guesses" to detailed line-item estimates.

PROPS. Interesting items, such as plants, furniture, household effects, and sporting goods used to enhance a department or window merchandise display.

PYRAMID PATTERN. Any of a variety of display arrangements of books (arranged face out) or merchandise, with most of the bulk (titles) at the base and ascending in a stairstep manner to a single item (title) at the peak on display steps or tables.

QUALITY PAPERBACKS. Paperbacks published by a trade publishing house and sold under a whole copy return. (Also called trade paperbacks.)

RAMP. A gradual sloping floor surface, inclined from one gallery or floor level to another.

REMAINDERS. Publishers' overstocks sold at a new retail

price lower than the retail price of the books when they were first published.

REPRINTS. Books that are reprinted and sold at a retail price lower than the retail price of the books when they were first published.

RETURNS. Books or merchandise brought back to the bookstore for credit or exchange by customers.

SALES AREA. The space where sales are transacted, including cashier stations, service and information desks, and stockrooms.

SALES METHODS. One or more of the following popular methods of selling merchandise that may be used in the same bookstore:

Self-Selection. Merchandise is displayed on fixtures to encourage the shopper to touch, examine, and select items without pressure by sales personnel.

Self-Service. Merchandise is displayed on open shelves so that the shopper selects items from tables, steps, gondolas, or wall units without sales help. Very often, the customer must enter the area through a gate and exit via a checkout counter.

Over-Counter Selling. Merchandise is shown to the shopper by a sales person stationed behind a showcase or counter.

SALES VOLUME. The annual gross earnings at retail.

SCALE. All professionally prepared floor plans and elevations are drawn incremental to scales, such as 1/4 inch = 1 foot, in which, for example, the ratio of one-quarter inch on the drawing represents one foot of measurement in the actual project and its objects.

SCHEDULE. A written plan designating the beginning and completion of each step in the work of planning and building a bookstore from inception to the grand opening.

SECTION. A scale drawing showing a building or object as if cut in two.

SERVICES. All activities supporting the selling function within a bookstore.

SERVICE DESK. A counter arrangement conveniently located within the sales area to service the complete store. Designed to accommodate special order, telephone order, information, and will call functions. (Also known as an information desk.)

SKETCHES. Rough draft drawings made in a freehand technique that outline floor plans, elevations, sections, and perspectives. Sketches are used to explore several possible solutions to a store's specific planning and design problems and to enable the bookseller to visualize and evaluate these solutions.

SPECIALTY BOOKSELLER. A bookseller for whom greater than 50% of sales are generated by the sale of any one of the many types of books.

SPECIFICATIONS. A statement of scope, details, materials, methods, and performance of a bookstore building project.

STACKER BOXES. Wooden boxes designed to facilitate display build-ups. They are used both as platforms and to provide extra height for the displays.

STEP. A wooden display fixture used back-to-back or in conjunction with a display table. Composed of three steps with an overall height of approximately 30 inches and the width of a display table.

STORE PLANNER. An individual with a minimum of 5 years of sound professional experience in his or her chosen specialty, with a strong background in book merchandising, designing, planning, graphics, and a thorough knowledge of bookstore fixtures and features.

STYLE. A particular or distinctive character of bookstore design and decoration associated with contemporary and historic architectural and decorative themes.

TABLE. Any open selling fixture generally designed to contain book and merchandise stock, with the horizontal upper-surface being used for merchandise presentation.

TITLE DEPTH. The quantity of any particular title on hand or to be ordered.

TRAFFIC. The movement of people or goods through a bookstore, horizontally and/or vertically.

TRANSACTION. The recorded completion of a retail sale.

TREND. The recognition of the general directions of book and merchandise buying patterns early enough to take advantage of their sales potential.

TROMP L'OEIL. An eye deceiving, painted decoration giving a three-dimensional effect.

TURNOVER. A term for evaluating inventory calculated by dividing yearly sales by the average of a 13-month inventory.

TYPES OF BOOK BUSINESSES.
Independent. Not part of a chain or institution.

Single. One store location.

Multiple. More than one store location.

Institutional. Operated by a non-profit entity such as a college, church, museum, or government.

TYPES OF SHOPPING AREAS.
Downtown Metropolitan Shopping Area. Urban area; one must exit outdoors to enter another store; stores are close together.

Local or Regional Mall. Stores are attached and enclosed; possibly containing one or more full-line department stores; mall ranging from 100,000 to 1,000,000 square feet.

Free Standing. An area store not attached to any other store.

Strip Center. A series of attached stores on a main street or highway; one must exit to outdoors to enter another store.

Village Shopping Areas. Suburban or rural area; one must exit outdoors to enter another store; stores are close together.

UNDERSTOCK. The storage/display space underneath counters and display tables.

VALANCE. A horizontal member located at the top of a wall-height selling fixture, sometimes used for category signage and to conceal a continuous light source.

WALL FIXTURE. A section of fixtures attached to a perimeter partition for the display, presentation, and storage of books and merchandise. It may be an integral part of the partition construction or prefabricated, and may have an open or enclosed case.

INDEX

ACKNOWLEDGMENTS

PHOTOGRAPHY CREDITS

The author and the publisher would like to thank the many booksellers whose stores are featured in this book. Every effort has been made to obtain the names of photographers and copyright clearance. We do apologize if any omissions have been made.

The following credits are in numerical order as they appear on the pages of the book. Ken White is identified as KW, Bill Mitchell as BM, and Herb Nelson as HN throughout.

pi Kasparowitz; pii BM; p2 HM; P4, 5, 6, 7, 8, 9, KW; p10, 11 HN; p12, 13, 14, 15 KW; p17, BM; p18, 20, KW; p21, HN; p25, KW; p27, HN; p30, 31, 32, KW; p34, BM; p35 KW; p36 top, bottom, KW; p36 center, HN; p37 top BM; p37 center HN; p37 bottom, KW; p38 BM; p39 HN; p40, 42, 43, 44, BM; p45, KW; p46, BM; p47 HN; p49, 50, BM; p52, 53, KW; p66, 68, HN; p70, 71, KW; p74 left, BM; p75 left, KW; p75 right, Kasparowitz; p76, 77, BM; p79, 80, 82, 83, HN; p84, KW; p85, BM; p86, HN; p87, KW; p88, 89, 90, HN; p92, 93, KW; p94, 95, 96, 97, 100, HN; p101, KW; p102, 103, HN; p104, KW; p105, HN; p106, BM; p108, John Herr; p109, KW; p110 left, HN; p110 right, KW;

p111, HN; p112, John Herr; p113, KW; p114 left, 115, 116, 117, KW; p118, 119, 120, HN; p121, KW; p122 top, HN; p122 bottom, KW; p124, HN; p125 top, KW; p126 top, center, HN; P126 bottom, KW; p127 top, HN; p129, KW; p130 top, John Herr; p130 bottom, 131, KW; p132, p134 top, center, HN; p134 bottom, KW; p135 top right, HN; p135 top left, bottom, 136, KW; p141, BM; p144, 146, 147, HN; p148, 149; KW; p150, HN; p151, KW; p152, BM; p154, p155, p156, 157, 158, 159, KW; p160, 161, BM; p162, 163, 164, 165, HN; p166, John Herr; p167, BM; p168, 169, KW; p170 John Herr; p171, 172, 173, 174, 175, 176, 177, KW; Front Cover, HN; Back Cover, KW.

ARCHITECTURAL CREDITS

Bookstores which appear in the book that were designed by others include:

Academic Bookstore; Academy Bookstore; Black Oak Bookstore; Blackwell's Art & Poster Shop; Book - Friend's Cafe; Canterbury Booksellers Coffeehouse; Clean Well Lighted Bookstore, A; Cody's, Cooper Square Bookstore; Galleria Bookstore; Harry W. Schwartz Bookshops; Kroch's & Brentano's; Olsson's Books & Records; Powell's Bookstores; Moe's; Tattered Cover Book Store, Taylors; Yaesu Book Center.

ENDNOTES

1. Page 2, Chapter 1: U.S. Chamber of Commerce

2. Page 5, Chapter 1: American Booksellers Association, Inc., (ABA), 560 White Plains Road, Tarrytown, NY 10591, Tel.: 914-631-7800; 800-637-0037; Fax: 914-631-8391

3. Page 15, Chapter 1: American Wholesale Booksellers Association, (AWBA), 702 S. Michigan, South Bend, IN 46601, Tel. 219-232-8500

4. Page 15, Chapter 1: Baker & Taylor International, Ltd., (B & T), Five Lake Pointe Plaza, Suite 500, 2709 Water Ridge Parkway, Charlotte, NC 28217, Tel.: 704-357-3500; 800-775-1800; Fax: 704-329-8989

5. Page 16, Chapter 1: Diamond and Capital City Wholesalers; Diamond Comic Distributors, 1718-G Belmont Ave., Baltimore, MD 21207; Capital City Distribution, P. O. Box 5156, Madison, WI, 53708

6. Index: National Association of College Stores, (NACS), 500 East Lorain St., Oberlin, OH 44074; Tel: 216-775-7777; 800-622-7498; Fax: 216-775-4769

7. Index: National Association of Store Fixture Manufacturers, (NASFM), 1776 N. Pine Island Road, Suite 102, Plantation, FL 33322; Tel: 305-424-1443; Fax: 305-473-8268